The McJazz Manuscripts

The McJazz Manuscripts

A Collection of the Writings of

Sandy Brown

Compiled and Introduced by

DAVID BINNS

FABER AND FABER

LONDON   BOSTON

First published in 1979
by Faber and Faber Ltd
3 Queen Square London WC1
Printed in Great Britain by
Ebenezer Baylis & Son Limited
The Trinity Press, Worcester, and London
All rights reserved

British Library Cataloguing in Publication Data

Brown, Sandy
    The McJazz manuscripts.
    1. Jazz music   2. Brown, Sandy
    3. Jazz musicians – Great Britain – Biography
    4. Clarinettists – Biography
    I. Title
    785.4'2'08   ML3561.J3

ISBN 0 571 11319 2

Contents

Lucky Schiz and the Big Dealer

Sometimes I climb inside that room in my brain
And never want to see the outside again
I feel lucky inside
And I know I can win
So Dealer: Oh well well, let the game begin

My room is big but I can make it real small
Troubles on me I just pull in a wall
I feel lucky inside
I'm so cosy and free
So Dealer: Oh well well, I'm so glad you invented me

My eyes are open but I pulled down the blind
No evil photons creepin' into my mind
I feel lucky inside
Everything there is fine
So Dealer: Oh well well, they can't touch what is mine.

You think I'm crazy but it's you that's insane
You're runnin' scared cos you can't walk in my brain
I feel lucky inside
And I know I can win
So Dealer: Oh well well, let the World begin . . .

Music and lyrics, Sandy Brown, 1971

Illustrations

Photographs (between pages 110 and 111)

Line drawings

- 1 -

Introduction

One evening in the late summer of 1973 a small crowd of regulars gathered in the basement cavern of the 100 Club in London's Oxford Street. They had come to listen to another evening of inventive and occasionally sparkling jazz clarinet by Sandy Brown and his 'gentlemen friends'. At the end of the first session Sandy issued a familiar invitation through the comforting cigarette haze: 'Ladies and Gentlemen, we are now going to take a short break for some refreshment, and repair to the bar, where you are welcome to join us, but not, of course, at our expense.' Amongst those who took up the invitation was a slight, retiring vintage-motorbike connoisseur and publisher. Their conversation, ranging widely over jazz, literature, architecture and acoustics, stretched late into the after-hours drinking session.

A few days later, Sandy penned a note to 'Mike Bream', suggesting a lunch that his Aussie secretary would arrange. His recollections of the evening's conversation were accurate in all those details that had interested him, apart from an unfortunate confusion as to the name of his companion. The association with a freshwater fish was right, and this, together with the alliterative reference to two-wheeled machines, had created a new character. Had it not been for this chance meeting and the following lunch to lay Mike Bream to rest, Frank Pike might never have encouraged Sandy to write his autobiography. The synopsis appeared on his desk a few days later and read:

SYNOPSIS

1 GENERAL

The book is part autobiographic, part episodic anecdote and part criticism of jazz and pop during the last 20 years. The parts are intermingled in a 'carrier' narrative as follows:

11

In which I explain how I was compelled to direct the extraordinary career of Sandy Brown, the jazz clarinettist, into ways less destructive to us both than would otherwise have obtained: how we shared a room for six months at the age of twelve, and why I was forced to bar him from cohabiting with me ever again.

tells of Brown's excesses concerning well-established musical theory, his importunate advances to (often quite elderly) ladies and how I persuaded him, in spite of his indolence, to temper his aggression (which was not wholly dissociated from laziness). Some passages from Brown's own lips recount his jousts with famous musicians of the day.

Ronnie Laing, a famous mind doctor, diagnoses a problem and tries to kill me in order to save Brown. I point out his mistake and survive, but am taken suddenly drunk and assaulted by a loved one.

Brown accepts me: his terms are stern but his demeanour changes. I am now permitted to help him with his assessments of musical developments in jazz and the beginnings of pop. Happily he is prepared to pay almost any price for his freedom.

Chapters 5, 6, 7 and 8

comprise a bizarre history of ten years on the road with Brown's band which I was largely allowed to direct as manager. Numerous misconceptions about Trad, Mod and Pop are rectified.

Brown, mysteriously, takes a keen interest in my own career: mathematics abound and I abandon Brown's future as lost. I become famous.

I further my surge into architecture, acoustics and the internal workings of a mammoth broadcasting organization. Brown becomes preoccupied with ladies and gentlemen above his station, but takes no note of my recriminations. He has invented a new way of playing the clarinet which, as yet, convinces nobody. In a singularly coherent piece he describes what he is about and I also fail to dissuade him from this errant pursuit.

Chapter 11
recounts Brown's travels in Eastern Europe, the United States and elsewhere playing with the leading jazz musicians of the day. He renounces me completely and I lose control of his fortunes irrevocably.

Chapter 12
I ply a trade with disgraceful financiers whose misdemeanours are related in full. The protagonists are concerned with moguls including The Beatles, The Rolling Stones and the perpetrators of the most gigantic financial failure ever recorded in the field of studio design.

Chapter 13
The Monotony Club of Great Britain is formed, occupying many of my waking hours. Meanwhile Brown has started writing musical criticism. He has also found sanctuary in militant atheism.

Chapter 14
I discover the avant-garde movement, and, reconciled, discuss it with Brown, whose views I find as flippant as ever.

Chapter 15
I talk to Brown about the last twenty years of music in a question and answer dialogue which crystallizes his thoughts, but not mine. He is never evasive and I am always specific so the answers are clear-cut and final. Other authoritative voices refute these conclusions, however, and the reader is thereby encouraged to draw his own.

After this initial burst the project remained quiescent. Almost a year later, in August 1974, the architectural and acoustic practice of Sandy Brown Associates had grown to a point where its partners decided that their grave liabilities to each other should be placed in the hands of an insurance company. Sandy was summoned to the consulting rooms of a Harley Street consultant for a routine medical check-up. Having completed the probing of flesh and bodily fluids, the consultant took a deep breath and said, 'If I were you, Mr. Brown, I would consult your own doctor as soon as you can—this afternoon if possible.' Being in the service of others, he advanced no further details.

On a number of occasions over the years, creeping hypochondria had led Sandy to consult his West Hampstead practitioner with afflictions ranging from cancer of the colon to cirrhosis of the liver, all of which had miraculously disappeared. The result was a deep sense of mistrust on both sides, and prescriptions of the 'there's nothing the matter with you—get out of bed and back to work' kind. A sixth sense told him that this might be the real thing, and, having sought the advice of a further Harley Street practitioner, he found himself, during the early weeks of September, in Guy's Hospital being treated by one of the country's leading consultants on malignant hypertension, or high blood pressure. It was during these weeks that the autobiography was started and a steady flow of handwritten pages was pressed into the hands of visiting friends to be sped to the Bloomsbury office for typing. With the condition under uneasy control, Sandy was discharged and the writing stopped. The advice had been: 'Take it easy, Mr. Brown; slow down and let others take the load.' And they were prepared to, but Sandy had made up his mind not to relax his exhausting pace running Europe's largest firm of acoustic consultants, writing, composing, and most of all playing jazz. In retrospect I'm sure he knew from that day in August that his days were numbered. It was never allowed to show or be mentioned and bad days were passed off as hangovers and with jokes about bags of pills.

In a television programme made by Scottish TV in 1973 about Sandy and his work on the Edinburgh Opera House, Sandy claims to have computed the average life span of jazz musicians as 44. He joked, 'I'm 44 so I'm now living on borrowed time.' And two years later, on 15 March 1975, he was dead. In the same programme he was asked if he were to have a choice between being a top acoustician or the best jazz clarinettist around, which would he choose: he replied: 'Excuse my arrogance but do you really believe that I'm *not* the latter?' He went on: 'but one does have other commitments to consider: I have a wife and two lovely kids who have to be fed, and a musician's life, like a policeman's in the Gilbert lyric, is not an easy one, or sometimes a very happy one.' A varicose vein which might have given complications put Sandy in hospital again during the first weeks of June 1974. With interruptions only for essential office work, he poured out the manuscript almost without correction or rewriting. With the offending tube removed he left the hospital and the book, by this time about half complete, never to return to either.

The duality in Sandy's personality was discreetly disguised even to those who knew him well and observed him closely. It appeared to flow smoothly and encompass the polarized worlds of architecture and jazz, but it is in his writings that the conflict was most apparent. There were times when the shift of image could not wholly convince. As Sandy put either.

> Having two professions is quite an advantage for a physicist or architect: they think of one's outside interests as additional to one's talents. Nothing could evoke more suspicion among musicians. The word they've coined to describe people like me is 'semi-pro'. This is intended to and does make one feel awful— a half-professional. When I'm playing somewhere I keep stumm about my day-job—by the way that's another derisory term invented to describe wasted activities of semi-pros. This works quite well but never far from my mind is a story Wally Fawkes— Trog of the *Daily Mail*—told me about his own double life. It seems that other cartoonists think of him as 'the one that plays the clarinet', and other musicians think of him as 'the one that does the cartoons'. You can't win.

In his autobiography, the other self has a *persona*—Alastair Babb—a figure who will hear confessions and responds with reprimands and lectures. Searching through his files, I came across an undated piece in the style of an unidentified pastiche, which gives some clue to his literary origins:

> After studying the writings of Freud, Adler, Jung, Kierkegaard and Ronnie Laing ('studying' is perhaps putting it a shade strongly—I never spend more than 40 seconds on a page: some-times I don't like the look of a page, or pages, or even whole books, and consequently don't read them), I have almost eagerly avoided conclusions about human behaviour. When attitudes are struck in my dealings they invariably emanate from my patients, the only exception being a fragmentary allegiance to therapeutic and pleasurable activities evoked by my obsessive preoccupation with derision.
>
> I must tell you about myself. Almost nothing I say or write is true, in the sense that I believe it, but I am now writing quickly

15

without 'thinking' to give a chance for reality (if there is any) to appear occasionally and briefly through the massive defences I have built up to prevent precisely this type of prying curiosity about my affairs.

My methods may interest you. The mainstream of method is evident from the text. It is leavened with traces of a self-imposed ignorance of current psychiatric practice; but some further explanation is warranted at this juncture. It can be said (conceivably only by me) that if there is a common thread in psychiatric investigations it is a professional, rather impersonal or detached compassion. I use this mercilessly. My compassion, however, is unswervingly directed towards myself and away from my patients and their pitiful problems. Occasionally, too, the detachment slips away to reveal (as you will see) naked emotions such as boredom and apparent drunkenness. When this happens it is perceptible to all but my most withdrawn patients. Their obvious distress at such revelations affords me the keenest satisfaction condensed into such a short, compulsive pleasure explosion that self-restraint is unthinkable. These moments I call 'gestalts'. (It has been necessary, due partly to my incomplete grasp of intellectual concepts, and partly to my burgeoning arrogance to redefine many technical and metaphysical terms.)

You will notice in my method the use of semi-religious concepts such as 'good', 'evil', and so on, relating to all sorts of people, things and adventures. I use these because they have a certain currency even today. I do not use them discriminately, and you may wish to substitute one for the other in parts of my text to increase your understanding of posed situations. I assure you this will make little or no difference to my intended meanings, and if you wish you may prefix each with the term 'a priori'. In every case this will make sense. As an example, one of my patients (a junior member of the British National Party) whose bed-wetting had become an embarrassment to his Jewish mother, explained to me that A. Hitler was 'a good man' and M. Gandhi was 'evil'—adducing evidence of the autobahnen and the increased wog population. I have some reservations about this hypothesis, particularly in respect of those infuriating expansion joints in the concrete every ten metres, but I agreed with him, substituting in my own mind the argument that, while Hitler had only accounted for 50 million violent deaths, Gandhi has condemned 500 million Asians to an unpleasant lingering (if fairly short) existence *already*. I must add that I did not trouble to rephrase my patient's ideas for him, as his problem bored me enormously (indeed he was responsible for a number of cherished gestalts). The outcome was highly satisfactory: my patient (I shall call him 'P') was mentioned in dispatches by C. Jordan, promoted to Lieutenant, and the bed-wetting is much improved.

Some time after his death, re-reading the manuscript, I resolved to call up 'Mike Bream' to try to persuade him to publish it as it stood, together with a collection of Sandy's writings and the letters that had brought a smile to the lips of clients and friends staring, heavy-lidded, at their morning 'IN' trays.

Sandy was born on 25 February 1929 at Izatnagar in India, where his father, an engineer, was working on the design and construction of the railways. Home was in Wishaw, south-west of Glasgow, and it was here his father died. Sandy was six years old. His mother took the family, Sandy and his elder brother Jimmie, to Edinburgh, settling in Willowbrae Road. At the age of twelve, he taught himself to play the clarinet and in 1943 formed his first band with schoolmates at the Royal High School—Bob Craig, Stan Greig and Stu Eaton. Jazz at the Royal High was considered a deviation from the academic curriculum and only tolerable as an extra-curricular activity. Despite this, and because of Sandy's infectious enthusiasm, the school produced a remarkable number of outstanding jazz musicians, among them Al Fairweather, Stan Greig, George Crocket, Stu Crocket, Jack Duff, Stu Eaton and later Charlie McNair, who helped to make British jazz of the forties and fifties the best in Europe.

In a senior class with his more academically inclined brother was a second fiddle player in the school orchestra called Karl Miller. He was later to become editor of *The Listener* and to commission the articles from which the selection in this book has been chosen.

After leaving the Royal High and completing national service in the Royal Army Ordnance Corps in 1949, Sandy set up his first semi-professional band with schoolmates Bob Craig, Al Fairweather, Stan Greig and Dizzie Jackson. During this period he was apprenticed to several firms of Edinburgh architects, and claims to have designed over two hundred lean-to garages and participated in the prize-winning design for Lerwick town centre in the Shetlands. Studies at the Edinburgh College of Art gained him a Diploma in Architecture, and his curiosity as to why what he was playing on the clarinet sounded different in different places was explored under the acoustic tuition of Dr. Marion Ross.

Introduction

In September 1954 he married a local beauty, Flo Armstrong. Shortly afterwards, feeling the constraints of the local jazz scene, he applied to the B.B.C. for the post of Acoustics Architect, and moved south to London. Here he was to join Al Fairweather, who remained his closest musical collaborator during the late fifties and early sixties.

In the following years Sandy established himself as an international jazz clarinettist and an acoustic architect specializing in broadcasting and sound-recording studios. He was responsible in the late sixties and early seventies for the architectural and acoustic design of many of London's commercial studios, including Lansdowne, Chappells, Philips, and Trident; and these were to play a large part in establishing London as the centre of pop and rock music.

I met Sandy at a symposium on concert hall design organized as part of the 1967 Bath Festival. When we met again in London, he asked me to help him, on a moonlighting basis, with studio design and implementation. This collaboration continued until in late 1968 he was approached by record producer Shel Talmy, representing an American consortium, and appointed as architect for a massive four-studio film and recording centre on the site of the former Duple Coachworks in Hendon. On the strength of this, and an advance of £1,000, we founded Sandy Brown Associates and set up office in the ground floor front room of an architect's office in the shadow of the Post Office tower. The small room became crammed with architects, draughtsmen and secretaries as the project was rushed to completion. The site turned out to be a marsh filled with Second World War bomb debris and a massive brick and concrete structure rose on a forest of bored concrete piles. Without warning the demise of Hollywood came to rest in Hendon. Having spent £200,000, the American parent company ran into trouble and severed the U.K. subsidiary, leaving almost as much again in debts. Sandy took a bottle of Scotch and in an adjoining office borrowed for the occasion told the staff the bad news and gave them their cards. The firm managed to survive this near-mortal blow, and through Sandy's tireless efforts, returning as a prodigal son to Edinburgh whence he toiled through Africa, Europe and the U.S.A., acquired a leading position in the field of international acoustics.

There have been many words written in praise of Sandy's contribution to jazz and the jazz clarinet. He had a unique position in jazz, both as a composer and performer and as a designer of the acoustic enclosures from which he broadcast and performed. In these areas the roles of acoustician and musician were compatible as he could hear things that even the most sophisticated instruments could not. A van-load of measuring equipment was required to gather data on a tour of opera houses in Europe and North America. To form his own judgement at the end of each four- or five-hour session Sandy would stand downstage the empty hall, take out his clarinet and play the haunting opening passage of Mozart's clarinet concerto.

The tributes and quest to slot Sandy into the history of jazz continue. There is one that recalls for me the music of this passionate, sentimental, tough and complicated man. Miles Kington, *Punch* writer and *Times* jazz critic:

> Sandy created his own voice from the strict traditions of jazz clarinet; and what a voice—wild yet controlled, acid but generous, blues-drenched but passionate, spiky, ravishing—it flowed out like the magnificent up-dated sound of some piper from his native Scotland. At his best he has no serious rivals in the world. Nothing personal here; I have met him twice: on one occasion he was rude to me, on the other he spilt my beer.

That voice was captured on disc. His personality is reflected in the following pages and in the memories of those whose lives were fleetingly enriched by his acquaintance.

David Binns
London, 1977

ACKNOWLEDGEMENTS

My thanks for assistance in compiling the following pages are due to Flo Brown, for a wealth of photographs and advice, Brian Lemon for the music, Jackie McFarlane for clips from his treasure-trove scrap book, Alun Morgan for compiling the discography and for his encyclopaedic memory of jazz, to Lord Stokes, Sir Ove Arup, Sir Michael Swann, and especially Jim Godbolt for permission to use their letters and finally to *The Listener* for permission to reprint a selection of Sandy's articles.

- 2 -

Straightening Jazzers Out

INTRODUCTION

Approaching personality dislocations
Scatter senses.
Why weren't bulwarks raised
Gabions placed in time
Allies sought?
—Pertinent questions in defeat. And
Victors' jokes aren't as funny
As wounding.
I'd tend your lesions but
Mine too are legion and I
Haven't spittle enough to lick them,
And yours.
'And yours mate!'

I

In the crumbling hinterlands behind Notting Hill, Brixton and Kensal Green during the sixties an exotic machinery assembled on the streets. Beneath the bubbled flaking paint there was little, except the presence of balding tyres still clinging to wheels, to distinguish the rusting steel heaps from the sandwiched clutter of a scrapyard. From time to time the vehicles could be seen in erratic motion, spraying blue smoke from decaying tail pipes, black pilots aboard. Spade cars were owned by usurers exploiting blacks' poorness in a rich society, but that they *belonged* to blacks couldn't be in doubt, unmistakably stamped as ten years old, bulbous products by General Motors' and Ford's British offshoots. And they came in three tones, jade green, sweetie pink and, inevitably, rust. Simple variations were permitted: you could have pink tops with green below the chrome-lined waist, or the other way around; the rust chose its own locations. It was advisable, though hardly mandatory, to bedizen the wings with badly pitted portholes, fins or some other flummery. Headlamps drooped to expose browned sockets. Damage to the rear often extended beyond mere crumples and grilles were nothing short of sculpture.

The cars were seldom repainted after an initial burst of acquisition fever. In a year or two the tones mellowed. Matt instead of gloss.

Blacks like these colours. I've wondered whether being Anglo-Indian had anything to do with my dislike of them. You know the reaction—or ought to if you watched Hollywood psychiatry portrayed by German-Jewish refugees in countless movies—suppress everything reminiscent of your roots and hates become transferred to some aspect of environment just remote enough to demand an hour and a half of celluloid unravelment. Always unsure of everything, I still wonder about this and other half-plausible explanations, but never for long. The colours were also those of a dream which told me my life was changing irrevocably for the worse.

I was just twelve years old. I had already endured wet dreams: well, the dreams were endurable, not the consequences—stained sheets and recriminations, or, worse still, none. Surely everyone must have known: why they didn't tell me about it was worrying. Clearly they'd told everyone else. So I started masturbating—wet daydreams. This wasn't much safer as I had no keys to ensure privacy, just timing. How long did shopping take? How long would Mother be at the bank? Long enough for a wank? But I still got caught at it. Being bright didn't seem to help. When one of my mother's excessively genteel friends returned unexpectedly early from the chemist with pills to discover this agitated twelve-year-old holding his cock in the front room, I stuttered nervously, 'The earache got so bad I thought I'd take my mind off it, so I thought . . .' But to further this line meant introducing the enormous cast of my fantasy who were by now doing unspeakable things to each other. I think some were already dead, or would have been if alive in the first place.

She had averted her eyes after the first shock and now proffered the prescription, like a blind person, tentatively and inaccurately, almost to someone else, someone neither of us could see. Disconnected thoughts raced about through my humiliation, and it was some moments before I took the bottle from shaking fingers to release her. Unsteadily edging to the door, she left very quickly and was never seen again in our house, although I did glimpse her occasionally in the distance up and down Willowbrae Road.

The willows were really broken and ancient elms, the road having been named in the casual ignorance of natural phenomena common in

Edinburgh, and quite thick enough to hide behind. Alternatively I could take a tedious detour to avoid a meeting. I felt sure that the delay in accepting the chemist's package couldn't have gone un-noticed and that this had impressed her that I was a juvenile flasher as well, that I'd wanted her to look again. I told my mother only that she'd delivered the prescription and that I felt much better. I did: I'd finished the wank—although with some difficulty. I hadn't fucked my brother's wife like Onan (which was no crime in the Book), but my seed fell to the ground just the same, for which shouldn't I have been put to death? The unexplained détente with the neighbour must have been a puzzle to Mother as the friendship simply evaporated, but she never referred to it.

Relations with girls had been impossible in India. Mother was Hindu, turned Christian on marriage, and desperately wanted me to speak English, which I learned, screaming protests, with a thick Anglo-Indian accent. This was known as 'chi-chi' in the cantonments of Calcutta and Karachi, and its clipped vowel stigmata precluded contact on level terms with the English—or rather the Scots—who ran the railway. Father recognized the difficulty in getting me into the nursery school: he'd 'gone native' (everything to do with his 'mistake' was always in quotes), and knowing the rules believed that the pain of forcing an integration at expatriate nursery schools which abounded in cantonments would be too much for me. 'Fuck them', he would say. I was too young to understand he might mean 'Fuck me', for he knew it was his 'fault' really.

So I couldn't go to the Club, and, sitting on my pony, I knew, when other ponies appeared on the horizon topped with silhouetted tiny figures domed with nodding topis, that Bagallo would lead my animal in another direction. Retainers directing other ponies had their instructions too, so glimpses were brief, being governed by the curvature of the earth and the slight elevational advantage over pedestrians a kid has in the saddle. Maybe that's why God made the world round, so people could meet, get together, be friends, without being interfered with by outcasts and misfits.

Our family was like a small banyan tree whose branches arch to become roots: looking outwards was a painful business. We avoided it. We kept close to the ground, like the banyan.

The boats were more difficult. Going back home was an ordeal. None of us seemed to look forward to home leave, although here my father may have been acting down a bit out of sympathy for Mother and me. But he had to face one genuine disadvantage: his bull-nose Morris, the gleaming booty of his exile, was in Nagpur. This was his prize, his badge of rank. Perhaps that made him sad. Mother's race was a hang-up that kept her in her cabin on the few times she came on the journey. I was dark enough to have a serial fight in the kids' playroom. P. & O. ships were worst: the kids were stronger, but the City Line ships had a habit of breaking down in the Indian Ocean and that made the trip longer. One of the P. & O. ships was the *Rawalpindi*, from whose rail I hurled the only rocking horse on board when no one was looking. I'd never been allowed on it by the white kids. Having steel runners the weight kept it upright and it rocked its way into the distance through the spreading foam of the wake, and for all I knew on to some distant shore.

Years later on the embankment near Tower Bridge I came across an elaborate P. & O. gangway salvaged from the Atlantic where the *Rawalpindi*, by then an armed merchantman, had been sunk in a fight with the *Scharnhorst*, a Kraut battle-cruiser, in 1941. A plaque told the story of the unequal action. The plaque on the rocking horse which rots on the beach at Kerguelen (a French island in the Antarctic rain belt at the foot of the Indian Ocean, where there are no flying insects, only a funny kind of cabbage and Australian rabbits eating it) reads: 'Alastair Babb, half-caste, threw me into the sea from a great liner which subsequently limped into port with a complement of wailing white protestant children and a discomfited crew but no other casualties.'

Two miles under the spot where the gangway floated to recovery, if you could read spotted marine growths on steel plate like the dots on a Japanese colour sensitivity chart (in which case it wouldn't be safe to send you to war—your eyes would let your country down), the message where there IS no message says, 'They nailed pop guns on my deck and pointed me in the direction of shells that could punch through half a metre of armour plate. First the rocking horse, now *this*.'

Boats were hell going to India or coming home. It was best to feign dysentery and get out of the way in the sick bay, which was upstairs in most ships and had real windows you could look out of, not portholes. You could get your Bovril and water biscuits and the tea with Carnation milk there in peace without having to scuffle about while Dad snored in a deckchair.

The one I hated most was *The City of Nagpur*, which cast its only propeller two days out of Bombay and drifted about for what seemed weeks. When I got home I *did* get to a nursery school and tried to draw that ship on the blackboard. I ran into a time/size confusion and asked for more board: the parallel chalk lines of the sea and the gunwale ran along to the edge and had to stop: I'd hardly started drawing the boat.

Home was in Wishaw, part of the smoky conurbation south-west of Glasgow, where Hamilton and Motherwell jumbled together under the shadow of Colville's steelworks. Nearly everyone worked at steel or coal, but a minority drove or conducted the trams, and, after they vanished, the blue Alexander's buses which took their place. Sometimes these reached Glasgow at the foot of the fertile Clyde Valley, where sulphur dioxide and hydrogen sulphide seemed to do no harm to the plums and apples ripening for juvenile theft in the orchards. The polluted atmosphere only smelled of rotten eggs if you were coming back from somewhere, so used were noses and taste buds to corrosion.

One stay, when I was six, was longer than usual. It lasted thirty-six years. Mother was home too for once, and suddenly began conducting a bus. Father was becoming more 'wrapped up in his work'. (The quotes are mine, and on this occasion don't indicate another misdemeanour with a black lady. There were to be no more.) He seldom left his room where he wrestled with papers, often in bed. I had no idea he was dying: he gave no sign, and I looked for none as he gradually withdrew from life.

From nowhere, it seemed, a coffin had arrived, and Father had vanished. Everyone in Father's large female family arrived crying and I was forbidden to enter his room. Nor were questions answered except with sobs. Mother was more stoic. She wouldn't answer, but shook her head slowly, as others would to indicate 'no'. With her that meant I could do what I liked. I could have my Saturday penny on Thursday. I needn't have a bath. I wasn't to get a sherricking for being rude in Hindustani to Mrs. McLaughlin. I opened the door to Father's bedroom and saw the box. I remember being surprised that it was supported only on ordinary trestles like a house painter would use for papering the ceiling. Why wouldn't they put my father's coffin on something decent? On red velvet or black bunched taffeta? Organdie? Burlap?

'Pick the misfit material and put a cross against it. Then describe the trestles in your own words, boy.' 'Please, sir, they were rough and splintered from a thousand hob nails and the wood was grey with cement and plaster. The hearse was bright yellow but I may be mistaken, sir, because no hearse is yellow.' Tears sprang; I was answering Mr. Ironside, a not unkindly Latin master, and watering eyes were inseparable companions of honesty under pressure: not fear, not grief. Mr. Ironside wasn't unaware that nothing could now staunch the smarting eyes, for he knew me well; but kindness could do no harm: 'Kick for touch boy'—a welcome metaphor from the loathsome rugby game played at the Royal High School. 'I *thought* the hearse was yellow, and *was* mistaken.' 'Good, good boy.' In that Latin invention from six years later Ironside had no more usefully to do, so I switched him off. He hadn't pressed me about the colour of the hearse. I used other props to ask myself the same question. Why would a yellow hearse carry my father away? At six, doubt about it didn't rise. I knew the yellow hearse as certainly as I knew my daddy was dead, but the colour eroded with the years—I never saw any hearses that weren't black—while, on the other hand, everything confirmed Father's demise.

Honeystone and Phee sent Mr. Phee to lawyerize about it, so it must have been true. Mother cut out something in the papers about it. Father had certainly disappeared, and in his place (I found out later) was money.

Phee and Mother talked and papers were signed. Days passed, and Phee would come for more talk and signatures. At the end of a fortnight he would pat my shoulder on leaving. 'Well, young lad.' That was all he ever said, and I came, with practice, to finish the sentence either as a benediction—'may the good Lord in his wisdom make you ride a bicycle and swim'—filling important gaps in my physical accomplishments at the time—or as a promise of untold riches: 'your father has left you the famous Chowdhurai diamond.' This was as large as a number of differing fruits at various times, but settled down at plum-size when I really had time to think about it: I wanted my contribution to Phee's speech to be realistic.

As balance and buoyancy infused my pre-pubic brown frame astride bicycles and afloat in Portobello baths, the plum-sized diamond turned out to be release forever from the Bessemers of Motherwell. Father's death insurance provided more lower-middle classification than a mundane accountancy ticket with the Bengal and North-Western Railway could during home leave.

In India things could have been different, and would have but for Mother. Servants, a bungalow, big grounds with a kind of moat to keep the hyenas out, all that was all right. But, for us, no club, no evenings with the Massons, Patons, Robbs. These were *Father's* friends. No play with the Burra Kaisa Ucha Hais, the little white sahibs who bossed the cantonments all day when men were at the junction office and women were planning evening parties. 'Get my pony', they would command, and grown men, lean-limbed, brown and sinewy, would obey, while their own children tumbled over each other in huts out of sight and defecated, squatting in public like their

26

father would do if not forbidden by the spotless whites from the Scottish Lowlands.

Mother was a Hindu. She couldn't pass in a cantonment. Elsewhere, with her light skin, she could have been an Arab or a Jew. At other times that could have earned her a violent death, so the timing at least could have been worse. When this dusky lady's husband was said to be dead by a professional legal man who would pay her thousands of pounds if she only believed him, well, what kind of option was that? Alive he'd been kind: we'd been lonely. Death had tendered us a better-than-even chance. No one asked me if I believed the yellow hearse was black, but if the deal depended on it I would have given in over that too and said yes. Who wouldn't? Give Mummy thousands of pounds and I'll *draw* the black hearse with my daddy in the box inside it, and I won't go beyond the edge of the blackboard either.

But I wasn't convinced about any of it. It seemed reasonable (and certainly advisable) to believe my father was dead, and reasonable, too, to believe all the other details that fitted with other deaths I'd heard about or seen on the movies as I clawed my way towards puberty, black hearses included.

I'd read stories in girls' annuals about fathers who'd lost their memory and came back unexpectedly after a few years; the tales always disappointed because when Dad turned up there was never more than three inches of print left. Once Dad was back that was it: big hugs, dinner like Christmas and all O.K. Story's end. If it happened in the Kilburn High Road everybody in sight would have been hospitalized and the police reports alone would have been hard to boil down to fifty sheets of foolscap. But it *could* happen, and the daftness of ignoring the probably entangled consequences seemed less silly to a kid with no father than discounting the possibility of a dead dad returning at all. You have to be very careful what you believe—I learned *that* from *Girls' Annual* for 1935—very careful. And would you have to be just as careful picking your way through *disbelief*? Really it seemed not to matter where you put your feet, there, like treading through a minefield of lemon sherbet dabs. The worst you could expect was a sickly fizz should you tramp on one labelled 'God' or 'double entry book-keeping'.

Why would one colour be worse than another? I had to be careful about that, though. That mattered. How the colours went wrong, the spade green and coon pink, was like this: while I balled this cushion every day where we now lived in middle—well lower-middle—classicism off Willowbrae Road in Edinburgh I was frightened of

girls. At eleven years I feared nothing else feminine but girls: I gave
that cushion hell: fucked the arse off it. God knows it was feminine
enough. But real girls were a problem. For one thing they brought on
this odd dyslexia. I could say *something* in a girl-emergency, but only
using words from an early Victorian Anglo/Deutsch dictionary—you
know, where it says, 'If you have no ticket you must pay as if your
travel journey was from the very farthest place', and then tells you a
groat is fourpence. Without pressure, at other times, I could speak
normally with no girls around. There was the Brodie girl. At thirty
she looked like M. Bibendum the Michelin man, but at thirteen she
was the most beautiful thing you'd ever seen. She never liked me
much, and I don't think it was on account of my colour because she
went to watch the wrestling at the Eldorado every week and Bomba
from Borneo was one of her favourites: she used to wet her pants and
jump up when he got to that bit where he staggered round all dazed
from a hundred forearm smashes, and suddenly, almost by accident,
sat on his opponent's face (a special nearly copyrighted trick), leant
forward baring tombstone teeth and pinned wriggling arms with his
knuckles.

This girl's inseparable female partner for a time, who was already a
portent of the roly-poly pudding she herself was to become, would
crunch her barley sugar in alarm at this savage expression of
Borneoism and say of the suffocating loser: 'I wouldn't like to be him.'
She said this every Monday until the cumulative pressure of imagining
her face stuck up Bomba's crutch curdled her reason. Well, that's
what we all thought, because she disappeared forever, having gone to
live in Rosewell which was a forsaken mining village only to come
from. I was glad she went, but still wary of an approach to her
beauteous companion.

One night this girl, alone and angelic, left the West End Café as it
closed. I was with her. Well, it was just that I was leaving at the same
time like everyone else, but a wonderful opportunity looked to be on.
She'd left her scarf. A real job at last, Alastair, the power and the
glory. I rang the bell. Soon the manager released the Yale and opened
the door enough inches to show his Jewish narrowing eyes and
customary pretending-to-be-cross-about-impending-trouble expression. 'We're closed.' Now listen to what I said—no more than a typical
manifesto of my affliction. 'This scarf's lady: what colour.' (That was
meant to be an aside to the loved one, but the mix-up at the start
seemed to have locked my neck vertebrae in a forward position.) 'If
you close the door I'll get it.' 'We're closed.' I suppose I should have
been grateful at mere incomprehension, but I went on: 'Are you

destraining me?' 'We're closed.' And the door slammed. Not one of the gathering crowd of puzzled bystanders thought to ask what 'destraining' was supposed to mean because it was clear that I'd come ticketless from the very farthest place, and even if I'd had pockets bulging with groats to pay with my trousers would only have fallen down with the weight.

My heroine never spoke to me again. Perhaps she thought my English wouldn't be up to it. And the Manager barred me from the West End Café: I didn't get back until Sandy Brown's band was playing there and I was handling the business. Even then he made me repeat everything about the money as if being Anglo-Indian was more foreign than being Jewish. He didn't have anything to do with the money anyway: that was sorted out by Pete Chilver, then the best guitarist in the U.K. He'd left Ted Heath's band to marry a young lady called Dominico. The Dominico family owned hotels in Italy, and, for obscure reasons, the West End Café as well. Pete paid Sandy's seven-piece band nine pounds for a Sunday night. 'If Sandy was drawing them in like Artie Shaw,' he said apologetically, 'he could have ninety.' Or was it nine hundred? Anyway it wasn't Pete's fault. In Edinburgh if Artie Shaw did the gig on percentage he'd have made nine. All these Scotch jokes about money are true in Edinburgh. No one there will buy anything except whisky and lemonade (the *real* Scotch drink). They can't even afford anywhere civilized to put it after they've finished with it: no sewage plant. The contents of half a million bladders and bowels are dropped a few feet out in the bay. Good mackerel fishing for free thinkers about recycling waste. Well the West End Café incident really finished me with girls for a bit. I'd have to go to speech training.

So a year later found me running hell-for-leather away from some twelve-year-old Amazons led by Eleanor Fairbairn in Northfield Circus. I had to jump a one-foot high fence for a clear round, but failed and crashed heavily to the ground, breaking an arm.

They put it together at the Infirmary, took the X-rays and sent me home. You took your chances at the Infirmary in those days, if you survived the wait: all day was average. Soon (about a week later, which *was* soon for free medicine in 1941) they wrote our G.P.: 'If at first you don't succeed . . .' This time they had to cut it all open, break it again and join it another way. Like these Japanese puzzles: you *know* there must be a right way because you remember seeing it together in the first place, so keep trying at it. They put a mask on my face and I felt like a sheep: with the muzzle my face was sheep-shape. I was being dragged round Northfield Circus round and round and the rope on a central winch pulled me into the pigmy fence which grew and changed from black cast iron to white-hot steel. All the colours were getting brighter and the fence was scraping my arm (leg? Please, Mr. Ernest, my little leg hurts and I can't untie the rope with my little hoofs . . . baa), but I could still talk, so dipping once more into the German primer for panic usage I shouted (mumbled) through the anaesthetist's cup, a leather thing you could throw dice in, 'I'm not perfectly asphyxiated'. Which must have caused a stir, if not alarm, in theatre B annexe. The pain got worse but I could no longer speak through the mask, presumably by now being perfectly asphyxiated. The fence was making a loud buzzing noise. Too loud. I saw the yellow hearse in the distance and was sucked under the fence. I then saw the purpose of the circus ring. It was to destroy me. It would do this without telling anyone how. Not Mother, not the powerless sheep who was Alastair Babb. Now I saw only the two colours, pink and green, the round moving belt I lay upon was green, the cavern I was to enter had pink jaws. Slowly the belt carried Al Babb, dago, to undefined destruction.

I was to have the dream a thousand times, and the punishment never emerged. Was I to be crushed as if the hole was the opening into the wave machine at Portobello pool? I tried to relate it to real violent ends in later years, but couldn't match the terror. The pink and the green spelled a doom not identifiable or even available to any world others lived in.

So I was right: you have to be very careful of what you see, what you take for granted, touch, feel, accept, but most of all what you make of all these senses. It goes without saying that no one else can make *quite* the same of them, except in girls' annuals, but here, without warning, *there was no one else around* to make any assessment of any kind. Just the carrier in green PVC, the receptacle in pink, the inescapable foreboding, and the buzzing noise.

You couldn't call it a nightmare, for when I woke I was still in the world of the pink and green machine. The device itself had vanished, but I knew it was lurking about somewhere; but what I could see, feel, hear and all that was still just a headscape. Well, what else can I call it? Everything was between my ears, behind my eyes, inside my skull. I could draw it for you: eyes out front looking at people or whatever, ears at the side listening, mouth talking perhaps—how would I know —and the real world in between.

This caused enormous physical difficulties with scale. If you see a building—a really big one like they keep moon rockets in—and put nobody beside it in the picture, it could be a matchbox. When I went to see Buddy Rich's band at the Odeon Hammersmith in 1971 the backdrop was supposed to look like skyscrapers. ('What do they have in the U.S.A. Mr. Artist? This is an American Band, remember.' 'Why, skyscrapers.') But for their size they would have to be at least two miles over the horizon. On reflection there wasn't a single thing the backdrop could represent, although it screamed realism. Eventually I settled for a view of the locker room in the engine sheds at Cowcaddens. Of course this made Buddy and the rest of the boys about seven inches tall, but they had their backs to the evidence: didn't know about their deformity. And it was no hardship to me. Thirty years previously I'd had to get everything into six inches by four, inside my head. This meant changing the sizes of everything all the time.

If you climb to the top of Arthur's Seat (922 feet equals 3 inches) you can see Ben Lomond on a clear day (50 miles equals 4 inches). I adjusted to that well. Soon it was easy to change sizes. I had to change colours too—easy. Ben Lomond was blue and it was only four inches away. Other hills four inches away were green. None of this scene was any trouble at all. What *was* worrying was this: what was going on outside? On the other side of Ben Lomond or outside the wall of the room or beyond the edges of vision? What were they doing outside my head? Worse: what was *I* doing out there? Was that where I was: still lying on the pink and green carousel? It was a waste of time looking at this stuff inside my head: it only *looked* like what I'd seen on the outside before they turned me into the sheep. It only *sounded* and *felt* like it. But it wasn't anything but an elastic perspective I'd invented to curtain off the unbearable reality of existence. What really mattered was elsewhere. Not far but unreachable. I was frightened by the proximity of it all as much as anything. A man's skull is thin like paper at the temples. On the other side of that drills were going, radios playing, Buddy Bolden's 32-foot exponential cornet calling his children home across Lake Ponchartrain. And the pink and green mincer that made a loud buzzing noise under the anaesthetist's mask. I couldn't hear any of it. Everything was terribly wrong and my foreboding made me shake all over at night.

Sometimes I would creep downstairs in our spacious semi, before Mother went to bed, for a cuddle. I suppose this was usually about nine or ten o'clock. Occasionally one of Father's relatives would be there talking. They would be told I was 'nervous' or 'suffering from nerves', whereupon varying advice was proffered. The cuddles stopped me shaking, but any other suggestions from outsiders on how to alleviate my suffering were both irrelevant and impertinent. I'd brought all these facsimile inhabitants of my headscape inside *myself*. What could they say or do to help? I knew it all already and had put the words in their mouths. They weren't the outside people: they were me. I'd heard none of the words before, I neither controlled them nor forestalled them, but I knew them. They were part of the protective me who could shut out the clangour of disaster with paper-thin bone. If only the protective power had been strong enough to stop me even thinking about the real ones outside.

Back at school I saw more facsimiles and gradually the paralysing fright diminished. One day in the playground I met a boy my own age in a mirror, wearing a home-made bow tie of velvet. It was enormous. This was Sandy Brown, whom I later brought from the inside out: he was the only one I invented to people the room in my head, although I tried often enough to make up others. 'How can you have trees and stuff in a room four inches square?' he said. He was to stay with me for thirty years, but I have to admit he got away from time to time, as you'll see. It will seem that I was always with him. Certainly I loved him. We were only what many others would like to be, lovers, but the shared room with the hundred-foot dwarf trees, the distant– close hills and the unknown fear was our only rational bond. The ontological ligature was, however, eternal.

It had been decided to hold mock elections at the school. If the idea was to teach the pupils about the politics of control or manipulation, the sort of thing that runs the world, the whole operation was a miserable write-off. But a valuable lesson which largely went unnoticed (and would have earned cancellation of the charade if it had attracted any attention from authority) was how indistinguishable creation is from copying. There's nothing wrong with that except that everyone teaching in this century keeps trying to compel teachees to think for themselves and then believes that they do.

I can't remember who won the election, but it was someone safe like the school captain, and the party he led to triumph at the hustings was simplistic right-wing conservative. The labour candidate also did fairly well for the following unsurprising reasons: although the Royal High was a fee-paying school, there were so many endowments from centuries of tycoon-fed compound interest that only half the pupils needed subs from parents: bulging coffers spawned scholarships that drew all sorts of clever riff-raff from the mining villages around Edinburgh. Sons of the Lothian coalfields socialized with socialism.

Sandy's florid bow tie was well in evidence, there being hardly anyone in attendance at his meetings to obscure it. Nevertheless, considering his own lack of interest and lamentable absence during much of the frenzied stumping, he was quite proud of the three votes cast in his direction. His party, the nihilists, had a singularly unattractive and flaccid programme. This was (as it was agreed dogma that no outcome mattered) promulgated as instructions to do nothing whatsoever—'Not as a protest, dear voters, but as a positive and determined policy', added Sandy to a small gathering whose only interest was to wonder how long anyone could get away with wearing a gaily coloured velvet bow tie instead of school uniform.

Soon after this, further sartorial impudence emerged. Dougie Monteith, who modelled himself on John Dillinger, grew a pencil-line Frankie Trumbauer moustache—something of a feat at thirteen—adopted a Capone-era silver fedora and the game was up: school uniforms would be worn. Monteith's control of quasi-illegal activities at school became legendary and he appropriately joined the police force on leaving, controlling unruly traffic at the foot of Leith Walk.

Sandy's positive and determined policy of inaction was betrayed in the campaign by what, for him, was unaccustomed industry: he wrote a song. This being neither catchy nor original (it sounded suspiciously like 'Where Did You Get That Hat') appealed to neither pupils nor masters. The lyrics, also composed by Sandy during an English period as an official chore and therefore escape from parsing some unparsible Henry James, expressed nothing more than an entreaty to support the nihilists at the poll. No reasons were adduced to the plea, no promises given nor opponents berated for malfeasance (an indispensable plank in other platforms). In fact the song was so tedious and lifeless that one pedantic supporter (Jimmy Balderstone, who claimed a hand in writing the melody while denying knowledge of 'Where Did You Get That Hat' and/or, as an alternative defence, that such a song existed at all) looked up 'nihilism' in the dictionary and demanded that some masters be killed, or other similar violent action 'like the nihilists in Russia'. But Sandy and I held to the philosophic meaning, approximately: don't believe anything your senses tell you unless it hurts not to.

For six months Sandy and I had every reason to support this interpretation of unreality. When we were strong enough to extend the negation to disbelief of tangible fear (the infernal spade-coloured machine waiting outside our cranial bed-sitter) we cheered up considerably and took to visiting the milk bar in St. Andrew's Street at lunchtime where it was thought you could feel girls from Gillespie's Academy. This was untrue, but was a popularly-shared wanking concept in the Royal High's dungeon-like toilets. The election lost and forgotten ten years later, Sandy wrote 'Nothing Blues', the lyrics of which reiterated the unassailably harmless unpopular and unspecific sentiments we learned, by rejection, from girls' annuals.

During the election Sandy Brown seemed to need looking after as much as I did. We made no pact. I took him on rather like stores for a journey, for I had composed his catalogue of belongings and attributes to carry with us, out of the room in our head or perhaps in the event of failure to reconcile us to a companionship inside it: I didn't care which. I thought either would stop me shaking. The cuddles were becoming embarrassing.

For the record, the nihilists were Jimmy Balderstone, Dan Gilvray, Sandy Brown and me. Later Karl Miller, a rough scholarship lad who took up literary pursuits, claimed to have been one of the group, but he also claimed to play football, thus proving untrustworthy in early middle age.

Don't let anyone tell you hallucinogenic potions are fun. The Royal High's hallucinatory hustings marked the end of a six months' bad trip for Sandy Brown and me, and that was non-stop every minute of every hour. Neither of us ever discovered who invented the other, nor do I, at least, want to, but we needed to do it whichever way round it happened. Of course, you won't find the name of Alastair Babb on the passenger lists to anywhere (except possibly Czechoslovakia after the tanks moved in: they're still looking for him). Sandy made the name up, and I used Sandy's as a swap deal like we might have done with 'Horrors of War' cards you got with bubble gum. If you had two of the one with Abyssinians' dismembered legs and arms with the ends dipped in ketchup and Mussolini's biplane stuck in near the top you could trade it in for Japs beheading Chinks in Manchuria. Getting a set of two was all Sandy Brown and Alastair Babb were about. Once we'd got it we left our room forever, and I forbad him from living with me again. The scenery didn't change much, but it was outside, not in, and things could be the right size again.

II

Have you noticed how many girls take up the clarinet? You don't often see them doing the Mozart, but there's always a few in the second and third chairs of the symphony orchestras. Of course, girls take up all sorts of other instruments too: in the brass band country round Leeds they play cornets and euphoniums and often turn out quite creditably in talent contests. A memorable confrontation was between one tiny lass who ripped off sixteen bars of triple tonguing on the cornet and was questioned about it by Huw Wheldon, not then

Managing Director B.B.C. Television but compère of a kiddies' TV show called 'All Your Own' where youths built dangerous moon rockets, bred tarantulas and generally showed the kind of inventiveness that would foster successful sensationalism in future years. Wheldon's public school English showed encouragingly effusive Welsh inflections: 'Good Heavens, that's really wonderful: I don't suppose many girls your age can play the cornet as well as that. How on earth did you learn?' 'Me Dad plays.' 'But you're still at school: when do you find time to practise?' 'After me dinner.' 'But you must have homework to do—and what about bedtime?' And so on. The interview continued at cross purposes for some minutes, Wheldon plainly unaware that 50 million inhabitants of the U.K. eat their dinner in the middle of the day: he was marked for high office. He wouldn't have been much good in a low one.

But clarinets are much more usual for girls: it's a straightforward blow job, after all much better practice, one would have thought, than horses, which some of them are always on about while fumbling their way to womanhood.

It's all a gamble though. Look at it this way. Suppose it was 1960 and you wanted to be rich and famous by appearing in TV Westerns, a girl who could ride a horse, side saddle and all, would have a big edge. A girl carrying a clarinet about would just look like a poltroon: 'Beggin' yore pardon, ma'am, I shore hate to ask this but some sidewinder shot ma hoss and I lost jest about everythin' else in a poker game: now all I have left is ma geetar and ah was shore hopin' yode spare me a job on yore ranch.' 'Why certainly, Mr. Cowpoke: be here at the corral with your instrument at 7.30 sharp. We're doing the Pavane for guitar and clarinet by Alan Hacker.' Whereas in the 1890s a busty Western actress with a clarinetic experience could go down to Geronimo or Sitting Bull and become a big star, especially if she sucked with forked tongue. Luck of the game.

When Sandy Brown started learning the clarinet in 1941 the chances of becoming rich and famous *his* way were remote: not that there weren't rich and famous clarinet players then. There were never more—Benny Goodman, Artie Shaw, Woody Herman. It was Sandy's determination to be untutored that sealed that avenue. It was bound to come out differently without lessons, and as if that weren't enough, Sandy's choice of a model was Johnny Dodds, who had died in August 1940 and was never rich and famous. Dodds himself had taken lessons in New Orleans from Lorenzo Tio Jnr. although it never sounded much like it. Tio and Daddy Tio came from an old tradition of Creole clarinet players and teachers and it's hard to relate the work of most of his other pupils: Jimmie Noone, Albert Nicholas, and, above all, Barney Bigard, to that of Dodds. Tio, Alphonse Picou and the other first generation jazzers in New Orleans employed an almost legitimate tone if a rather fiercer attack than symphonic players. One assumes that Theogene Baquet whose son George started playing professionally before 1900 was similar, but Dodds, George Baquet and Sidney Bechet (also a Tio pupil, but after a period of self-teaching) played in a fashion so far removed from the normal run of New Orleans clarinet that the genesis of the breakaway style must remain a mystery.

To describe it: it was the opposite of mellifluous. Every register was harsh and tortured. Dodds's control, however, was considerable, and somehow he infused a fullness to the centre of his tone so that the end result was not unlike Johnny Hodges's alto sax in timbre, although of course the vibrato was much wider and faster. But Hodges gave almost the same illusion, working, as it were, from the other side. His tone sounded almost sweet and bland but had a hard, nearly cruel superimposition of edginess. Dodds started with the edginess out in front. Eventually it was to take over completely in the 1940 recordings just before his death. Critical opinion is unanimous that these record-ings are inferior in quality to any others made during his lifetime. Sandy was convinced they were his best work: out of tune, accom-panied by the failing trumpet of Natty Dominique and squeaking like a loose board. Sandy would play the record over and over: 'Red Onion Blues' on one side and 'Gravier St.' on the other.

This unquestionably accounted for some part of his unusual approach to the instrument. Dodds was never excellently imitated but Sandy's copy was easily the best. Some other versions could hardly be played in public without spontaneous bursts of uncon-trolled merriment. At that time there were hundreds of self-taught musicians about: skill was short or not even available at all. Coupled with this, the copies were being attempted by middle-class European whites whose grasp of anything to do with African music was im-possibly tenuous. It consisted of a few records, perhaps a hundred, mostly of similar stuff: Afro-American early jazz, and although a number of geniuses like Louis Armstrong and Duke Ellington were involved, they could hardly establish a vernacular for lads whose future aspirations were Oxford or the Sorbonne. In some individual cases things improved a bit but in the main they didn't. The whole thing happened again ten years later with rock 'n' roll, and it will happen again, unless or until African music becomes recognized as a rather importantly permanent feature of culture.

Returning to the Dodds copyists, there were Alex Revell, Cy

Laurie and Sandy Brown in the U.K., Claude Luter in France and Bob Helm and Ellis Horne in San Francisco. Laurie's attempt was inept but desperately sincere. It was also dangerous. As he played his travesty of Dodds's sweeping phrases he described them graphically with his clarinet, and if you played trumpet or trombone on either side of him you stood to get badly cut about unless nimble. Bob Helm had his moments: a solo or two in the plodding two-beat of the Lu Watters Yerba Buena Band showed originality and determination. He sounded nothing like Dodds but perhaps that was a mercy as nearly everyone else managed to achieve no more than a grotesque caricature. But if you searched for a thousand years you would never come across a serious musician (if that's the word) like Claude Luter. He had only one peer, a tiny chap called Joey Clark who tragically died young, owned a brown E flat clarinet and played with a comedy band called The Alberts. Joey's incredible expertise was never to hit a right note during any performance. Luter, however, was demonstrably a dedicated Dodds man and by all accounts had little international humour in reserve. It's hard to know where to begin describing him. He always played out of tune, usually flat, but when caprice descended upon him, sharp as well. Sometimes the vibrato was so uneven it sounded as if he was both flat *and* sharp. The timing of rhythm sections in his bands was so erratic that criticism of this aspect of his playing was unjust if not impossible. Uncannily he appeared to achieve almost exactly Dodds tone on record, so occasionally one got the feeling that a badly under-the-weather but real Johnny Dodds was revolving on a turntable that needed urgent attention from the refuse collection service.

The only copyists who dug Dodds's secret—and that infrequently—were Sandy and Ellis Horne:

> Joining Dots
> Johnny Dodds
> Contrived a leitmotif of line
> In what crevasse
> Between the brass
> Could Johnny make the notes combine
> A second time to be conjoint?
> It comes to pass
> His gifts align
> With counterpoint

There was precious little of *that* among his followers, who slavishly repeated Dodds's phrases out of context, just anywhere. Not just anywhere in the tune: anywhere in the world as well. It became hard in the early fifties to get out of earshot of a bad copy of Johnny Dodds accompanied by the wrong chords on a banjo. Almost your only hope was a bad, but slightly better copy of George Lewis and the right chords on a banjo, because George only used about three and was much easier to copy anyway.

Before leaving Edinburgh Sandy had taken to visiting elderly ladies and young girls: the first friendship was rather laudable. It was with the painter Anne Redpath, whose son and nephew I knew. I had started my architectural studies at the College of Art. Sandy came along for the chat. Anne loved a chat with youngsters who happened to be about. She would go right on painting. I remember watching her put a purple flower on a still life in thick water colour with such skill and complete certainty that I was astonished and slightly alienated: she talked right through it as she always did, answering idiotically naive questions. I was forever begging reassurance for Sandy's clarinet playing, which at that time certainly needed some. 'Why don't you shut up about it?' 'Well, why not? Chardin kept painting in a decadent age and produced, well . . . like a special kind of painting of his own.' 'Cobblers.' 'It's true.' You can see the primitive thinking behind this, and I often came back to it when we went to Anne's. She was pleasantly encouraging and the meetings continued over some years. Sandy tried unsuccessfully to get involved with a girl who eventually married one of Anne's sons. He was somewhat unlucky about girls then as he was already going bald at sixteen.

The next girl was even more of a trial, although lovable. Her sexual innocence, even for Edinburgh where 1940 Hollywood standards were thought risqué, was astounding. Upstairs in a crowded tram she managed to suffuse the entire male complement of the top deck with a rosy glow of embarrassment. Her gaffe was to say—and who could blame her simple purity for few Edinburgh females countenanced sexual connections in language—'I like holding sausages, big ones. Do you?' The conductor fell down the stairs and hurt his hand: no blood but perceptible palsy. Sandy muttered an excuse and tried to leave, but found the injured official in his way. Stu Crockett, who was helping me with the band management, was sitting in front: he tried to read the advertisements nonchalantly, but found the ones he was looking at were backwards, being aimed at customers on the street.

So big sausages continued to be held in girlish Scottish hands while puritanically strictured shy cocks flaccidly flopped about like blanc-manges behind stoutly-fashioned fly buttons that felt as big as willow pattern plates in an emergency. 'Oh what a terrible waste', I can say now: it couldn't even have been thought at the time without a clouded feeling of guilt. Just a question of time like the clarinet-playing ladies? Come to think of it, the clarinet-playing ones in the symphony orchestras aren't usually the kind you could see in 1940 movies, hand on hip, chewing gum at the Regal, while George Brent was asking important questions about the real heroine, but times change . . .

What I'd crudely been trying to put to Sandy was that he should play pure jazz and work hard at it. Now we know 'pure' jazz was always a meaningless term. All it ever means is that that kind of jazz (pure) doesn't have anything else but jazz in it. 'What kind of jazz doesn't pure jazz have in it, Sambo?' 'Why, *no* kind of jazz, Mr. Interlocutor.' It would be easier to define pure Silvikrin Hair Tonic. That doesn't have anything in it except Silvikrin Hair Tonic: we know that by definition. I don't have the formula right here in front of me with all the chemicals, salves, oils and stuff that go up to make Silvikrin Hair Tonic, and I don't think the manufacturers would give it to me because I might goof with too little or too much of something and make *impure* Silvikrin Hair Tonic, which would make everyone's hair curl (if that's what it's not supposed to do using the *pure* stuff) almost as much as impure jazz—if you could find it.

We had all sorts of labels in those days: I don't think you could find the bottles they were stuck on now. One night Sandy's band— the one with Al Fairweather, Tony Coe and Tony Milliner in the front line, so it was one of his best—was playing at some trad-mad club. We didn't play trad of course. We had names for all of these clubs where poor receptions for banjo-less bands were mandatory. Dragenham was pissed Ford workers and not too many of *them* either. Ching-Ching-Chingford was onomatopoeia for banjo fetishism, and we renamed Havant 'Can't' because the life seemed to have ebbed from the customers, along with the tide in the Solent.

Well it was one of these clubs, not too sure it wasn't Wellwyn, a name which needed no repairs, just pronouncement, because the bar guvnor there was one of those who fucked off at five to eleven into some unwinkable hidy-hole, leaving instructions that staff reply to requests for after-hours band drinks by appearing sympathetically distraught: 'If only the guvnor were here . . . I daren't on me own.' 'Well in' all right. Cunt.

During the interval this young German student came up to us at the bar. 'Excuse me,' (that was barely acceptable courtesy unaccompanied by the offer of refreshment) 'but what you are playing is mainstream.' (A term coined by critic Stanley Dance to describe any middle-period jazz he liked.) 'Zis is a bestard music.' 'How interesting.' 'It is neizer traditional nor modern. It is a mixdure of boas of zem.' No wonder they lost the war: Lester Young, Roy Eldridge, Coleman Hawkins, Duke Ellington and anyone else Stanley Dance liked had to invent bop back in the mid-thirties, ten years before Charlie Parker, Dizzie Gillespie and Tadd Dameron, so that they could stick it in a bowl and mix it up with George Lewis's music to make mainstream soup. I was about to draw attention to the anachronistic logic when Sandy handed me his clarinet and made an introduction. 'This is Mr. Al Babb. He's just a stevedore, a dusky stevedore working and singing all day.' (Remembered words from a Smith Ballew castrata song of the twenties.) 'You, being a kraut, will appreciate a bold new experiment. An attempted miscegenation by proxy. Unless you move away quickly he's going to stick my clarinet straight up your arsehole.' We returned to our drinks, and though the young Aryan left slowly, not at all as directed, we were well compensated by his puzzled and troubled mush. But it shows you the madness and inescapability of categorization. I was to discover how indispensable this procedure is in Town Planning and to use it many times unsuccessfully.

Eventually I nagged enough to break down Sandy's increasingly desperate opposition to practising the clarinet. He hadn't just been stubborn about it, more belligerent. When he could no longer conceal that the basis was laziness, he gave in and trudged up the Pentland Hills from Balerno with Dave Paxton, yet another clarinettist from the Royal High. (There were at least four more who became professional players in the same decade.) They found a wooden hut near the reservoirs so the physical detail as well as the concept of woodshedding was observed. I suppose you could call it pure woodshedding. There was certainly nothing else in it but woodshedding. They played pure jazz and used pure Silvikrin: well Dave did, Sandy was getting a bit thin on top.

Clarinet playing isn't too hard if you blow it quietly: it's really a quiet instrument, but it can be awkward in keys unrelated to the open one: B flat, which is why they have an A clarinet as well. But what's needed is a logical clarinet, and that's next on the list for Professor Brindley who invented the logical bassoon. The bassoon really *is* hard. You have to play all sorts of notes with your thumbs. This is only because, being a keyed instrument, and a very large one, linkages have to be complex to get the tone holes in the right place. Brindley, who's an amateur bassoon player as well as a physicist, decided completely to re-arrange the fingering by using solenoids to open or close the tone holes wherever they happened to be. He then gave a convincing demonstration of how easy it was to play the most difficult passages on the instrument. Sandy asked about the clarinet, but you know how it is, it needs a clarinet player to do it. Brindley will be be too busy showing up the virtuosos on the bassoon.

What Sandy was able to do was play louder than anyone else. (There's some doubt about Tony Scott: Sandy played with him in Prague and thought himself shaded by a few decibels, but in view of Sandy's arrest there he may have been a whit subdued.) You don't get any bargains at clarinet. You have to trade in volume for facility. Tonguing the instrument takes patience because it takes time to speak. Above a certain speed and power it's impossible to tongue at all. This, in itself, could be a handicap or an advantage. In Sandy's case at least it could be said that he played differently to anyone else, but always claimed that this was due not to originality but to a slyly undetected eclecticism. When he was given the *Melody Maker* award for the tenth year in succession (1970) he likened it to the cunningly backhanded citation for good conduct stripes in the army. These are issued, officially, for various lengths of time (stretches would be opposite) of 'undetected crime'. They *know* you're a criminal in the army, but not being found out deserves celebration and approval.

As Sandy spent more time listening to blues singers—Sonny Boy Williamson (the *original* one), Kokomo Arnold, Blind Lemon Jefferson, Leroy Carr, Joe Turner, Big Bill Broonzy, and to the Gospel groups— The Sensational Nightingales, The Five Original Blind Boys—than to clarinet players or other instrumentalists, the copies came through, but somewhat unrecognizably. It all sounded convincingly original: only the tone was. This came from trying to play terribly loud. It seemed that Dodds must have been loud. No one could tell from records. Grand Funk Railroad *are* loud, although inaudible without 230 volts and 7,000 watts. But Dodds must have been loud unaided. He had to be heard in the King Oliver band over two trumpets, one of whom was powerful young Louis Armstrong. So all the Dodds copyists tried to blow the insides out of their clarinets. Sandy had started with an Albert system, sometimes called simple system, as opposed to the adaptation of Boehm's flute fingering arrangement, though it's any-thing but simple. The Albert is usually louder than the Boehm and has an unmistakably full tone. All the New Orleans players used various versions of Albert. When Sandy switched to the Boehm he missed the tone so much he huffed and puffed until he got an approxi-mation. As for the notes he played, these were fragments cut from the archaic and modern blues and gospel singers, a kind of blues confetti stuck in the end of a kaleidoscope. You could switch it all round to get

41

a new and brilliant picture every time, just from a few old blues remnants. Same old stuff really, but a lucky new way to put them together. 'Put your eye to this, sir.' 'Brilliant.' Shake, shake. 'Now this.' 'Brilliant again, like the stained glass in a cathedral.' Amazing what you can do with a few odds and ends: a permutable catechism rather than a liturgy. Perhaps there's no real difference.

Joe Meek, a recording engineer—he made 'Telstar' if you can remember that far back—used an echo chamber about six feet cube. This, he said, gave him a 'cathedral sound'. All eight cubic yards of cathedral. Eel Pie Island Cathedral. Joe was queer, sensitive, and most of all unlucky, although not quite so unlucky as some he came in contact with. In shooting himself he managed to take an uninvolved caretaker with him: someone who just happened through the door at the wrong time. 'That was a bit of bad luck all round', thought the pop music business, whose stomach for sentimentality, bloated with half a century of corny lyrics, just found room for a mourning macaroon at elevenses when the news broke.

Sandy had three special effects he added to his scrambled eclecticism. Growling, a trick he taught clarinettist Archie Semple who used it continuously and well, is simply done. Sing through the instrument and it will growl for you: the acoustic reasons take some explaining but the effect is easy. Then there are terribly high notes, say two octaves above usual top C. You can get these by biting the reed. If you bite it in the right place you can get harmonics (which are very close together up there), so you can get any pitch you want by varying the pressure. The third trick is lip trill. No one else can do it on the clarinet and Sandy hasn't been able to explain how it's done. It's one of these things that's too easy and natural to explain. But this isn't a clarinet primer, and these are only tricks. The resultant imagery is no more than the sum of these parts. You only think they are, like Joe's matchbox cathedral.

Sandy had taken a liking, after the tram-girl humiliation, to an early-middle-aged lady with a flat in George Street. She had an English public school accent and was called Mrs. Willock. Mr. Willock was never spoken of. She seemed to have come upon hard times for her class, having to take in lodgers. These, too, young girls at Art College, were from educational backgrounds like Wycombe Abbey, and were little hardship to Mrs. Willock. I met her one cold blowy day in Queen's Street: we had met once or twice with Sandy. The cold had turned the skin round her mouth and chin slightly blue. Somehow this made her look as if she shaved, and contact, a kiss on the lips, would be scratchy and queer. A further drawback was the precise shape of that bit under the chin which wasn't quite right. It seldom is at thirty-eight. Her eyes and nose were wrong—beginning to sound like an ogre, no doubt—but in that rather attractive Jill Bennett way. The nose came straight out. Jutting. From eyes that were deep set. Pupils and iris equally dark so the seeing part looked enormous. Sandy followed her about for some months while pretending to be devoting his attentions to one of the girl painters. Either way it would have been the Mellors role, very unsuccessful on an Edinburgh stage, because Sandy's accent was quite broad and interests between young ladies and budding lower-middle-class jazzmen were disparate to say the least. Apparently nothing was happening at all. Mrs. Willock, Anne, went out with 'sailors', as she called them, from Rosyth. They weren't sailors, of course, but captains and lieutenants. Only a Mrs. Willock could have called them sailors. Sandy never made his attentions clear, probably expecting repulsion, which he received in any case from one of the two students, one whom in my opinion would never get fucked even by the Duke of the World due to inordinate reservations about class. He found, more by luck than connivance, that the other one wore black knickers, and that was about the extent of his sexual forays.

Mrs. Willock had grown-up daughters who suddenly turned up from school after some months: they were both attractive but horsey —always at the stables, that sort of thing—so Sandy, who was beginning to become game for almost anything in this pristine household, having lost out to admirals and the *Tatler*, gave up unequal equine opposition. It was obvious the fuck wasn't on. He took to swallowing the cotton-wool entrails of benzedrine inhalers and thinking at length, if not deeply, about what to do about music. Benzedrine keeps you awake.

If you aren't going to practise, technique arrives in a haphazard way, leaving great gaps of competence. A carrier like a string bag in which only articles of some considerable size are portable. The trick was to collect the right groceries. That took much thought. The process was reminiscent of one of Woody Herman's bands where nearly everyone was on heroin. Herman had some new arrangements done and at rehearsal the musicians would sit reading them snapping their fingers and grinning in appreciation. 'Great, man: these are just great.' No one would play a note.

During this period Sandy was playing in a Dixie band at the Oddfellows Hall. None of the music he played showed improvement; in fact there was some backtracking as he was changing from Albert to Boehm at the time. The interest at the Oddfellows was barely musical, but there was nothing dull about it. I used to manage the band, sell tickets and so on, and the affairs were quite well attended with Sandy's Band, and Archie Semple's (or later Alex Welsh's). It also became a troilistic battlefield. Edinburgh had three gangs of youthful marauders. These were primitive societies compared to what later became ritualistic hierarchies formed by the violent bloods of the new estates near Glasgow where the Wee Cumbies, cub thugs, once humiliated the Big Cumbies, whose honour wouldn't allow them to bully their babies, by threatening to do battle to recover money stolen from the Middle Cumbies who, being cadets, were suitable bullying material. The Edinburgh gangs in the late forties had none of this stratified sophistication, but they had their moments, mostly at the Oddfellows Hall during the Jazz Band Balls we ran.

The three gangs were Golly's, Naz's and the Val d'Or boys. There was actually a Golly, who always smelled of gelignite—it has quite a strong, unmistakable smell—a Naz, a portly little chap called William Nisbet, and the Val d'Or was a café. Sometimes the leadership and even the names would become blurred or changed, but at every dance there was violence. We coined the phrase 'faces are changing at the Jazz Band Balls', some of them, regrettably, almost unrecognizably. We tried a different venue to give the gangs the slip but this attempt, held at the Palace Ballroom at the foot of Leith Walk, generated the most spectacular fracas of all. At one point Golly threw Naz down a flight of steps which ended in the centre of the dance floor. Al Fairweather, Sandy's trumpet player, tried unwisely to separate them and was lucky to escape injury. Then Naz lifted Golly and threw him against a mirror that covered one wall. One minute there were these two identical chaps hurtling towards each other back to back with a complete circle of onlookers open-mouthed and alarmed frozen expression: then crash! Half of them disappeared and the floor was covered with shards of silver. I found a pocket book before the police came with eight pence and a card proclaiming that a William Nisbet was unfit for army service. I threw it out of the window.

After that we hired two bouncers, both jazz fans, and things got quieter. One was Jackie McFarlane who was five feet tall, insisted on singing 'Frankie and Johnnie' in a nasal Dalkeith accent and learned his brawling in the International Brigade in Spain. The other was Tom Connery, who became Sean. None of his 007 crap ten years later matched the mayhem available from Golly and Naz.

III

A hundred years ago Hampstead Heath became, instead of just part of the countryside surrounding London, an isolated park. The railway got to Golders Green and housing kept nosing round until only early preservationists stood between the Heath and Victorian or Edwardian brickwork. Gradually, as the more desirable areas just north of the other park, Regent's, became swallowed in stucco at St. John's Wood, and as Bedfordshire redbrick crept down the hill from the edge of the Heath, pressure outwards from the old Roman Watling Street, the Edgware Road, pushed out lateral feelers from its stretches through Maida Vale, Kilburn and Cricklewood. The tentacles inevitably met in the centre. The fields here were owned by the Maryon-Wilsons, a family with strong ecclesiastical leanings. These godly precepts, while benevolently intended, interfered to some extent with a logical businesslike approach. Some parcels of land were delivered freehold to developers, others had varying leases attached, and it would be easier to describe the residual property tangle as something that just happened, than to look into motives which no doubt seemed like a good idea at the time but of whose consequences almost no sense could be made.

This was West Hampstead, or, for Protestant whites (about 50 per cent of the local population), British West Hampstead. The boundaries of the district are vague. Although there is a South Hampstead station no one really accepts that as the name of a district, so the approximate limits would be Boundary Road (with St. John's Wood), Finchley Road (with Hampstead proper), Mill Lane (with Cricklewood) and Kilburn High Road (with Brondesbury and Kilburn). The confines of the Maryon-Wilson estate, however, are much smaller, centring on Greencroft Gardens with a number of parallel streets and two cross ones. The streets are long, about half a mile, and, while the total population of West Hampstead must be about 20,000, that of the estate itself isn't inconsiderable at about eight thousand, mostly bed-sitters. The largely Jewish developers were surprisingly flamboyant in choice of design, bearing in mind their frugal reputation. Much wrought iron wove in stars of David. Carved brickwork and turreted, gazebo-like structures commanded the heights. The only concession to parsimony was the reversion, once round the corner from the façades, to London stocks from the brilliant red facing bricks shining scrubbedly to the streets. The glowing colour of these bricks— a red often used in illustrations to science fiction literature of just-above-interplanetary Arthur C. Clarke level, is renewed by an automatic meteorological process each year. The bricks are porous and as the water soaks in during the winter and freezes the expanding ice pushes the old faces off: a kind of moulting. The renewal is now in its seventieth year, and on average about half an inch of brick has gone. In some cases much more. But about seven o'clock on a summer evening the colour's worth it. The London stocks are grey and yellow, hard as flints and dependable: great value for money, but there's something heroic about annually reborn brickwork.

Eight thousand people: a not-so-small town. There should be a happy family of tradesmen, a butcher, a baker, a candlestick-maker. There's nothing. Worst of all there are no pubs. Whether the Maryon-Wilsons' religious scruples forbade John Barleycorn or whether the profitability of drink in a largely Jewish community was considered dubious will be hard to establish now. But there it is: a boozer desert. In such circumstances, how did jazz musicians settle here in quantity? This was no place for them in socio/economic terms—high rents, cramped accommodation, insuperable problems practising instruments three-inch-partitions-away from sleeping families. And no boozers for miles. The overriding influences on the choice, so important as to dismiss all other considerations, were being near town and the road North. Getting back to Sidcup or Cheam at four o'clock in the morning after a gig in Birmingham was something only to be undertaken until a bed, any bed, could be found in West Hampstead. At any time during the fifties and sixties, 100 jazz musicians would be living in West Hampstead, at least fifty of them seemingly at 4 Fawley Road, or Bleak House as it came to be known.

Outwardly there was little to distinguish the place itself from many other unattractive three-storey terraced dwellings. Well . . . perhaps it had a rather special *darkness*. Its environs were unusual if consistent. There would always be the burnt-out hulk of a motor car outside or across the road or in the near vicinity. The charred remnants changed from month to month: only the story behind the original was partly known. Tony Bayliss, a bass player, owned that and it had just gone on fire. Spontaneous combustion. Efforts to put it out failed, and like everything at Fawley Road it was left alone if no longer of value. Inside the house—the distinction between in and out was blurred by the door panels having been kicked in as inhabitants, lodgers, wayfarers forgot/lost/never had keys—conditions had achieved squalor of a surrealism it would have been hard to invent. The sink was no more than an exemplar. It looked like a microcosmic Mediterranean: azure blue water and peaceful. The calmness remained unchanged for ten months, as if the commune members were too sensitive to drain away this simple beauty. Dishes and cups would somehow be washed else-where, perhaps in a dust bath like birds, or more likely—for the Fawley society were ingenious and experimental—in Flash or some-thing that didn't need water or suds, or even, because emergencies often arose in the house, not washed at all, just reused, opening new avenues of flavour leaning towards jugged hare and long-hung game.

The story of the sink was at once less pretty and more complex. Legal Pete had started by being sick in it. While this was an improve-ment on being sick up the wall and waking everyone up, proudly 'Come and look at this: look how far I've got up the wall', Pete's diced carrots and tomato skins had been wolfed down without chewing between pints of Newcastle Brown and the aggregate being larger than usual, was too big to get down the drain. For some weeks dishes were piled in, the top ones being washed when required. It was never understood how, but Tony Coe, writing a score, managed to spill a whole bottle of blue ink on top of everything else. After that you couldn't see below the surface, and it became possible to believe, although only in Fawley Road, that an ever greater evil lurked there. You could get your hand bitten off looking for a plate: no agency disturbed the serene waters. This was a nuisance at parties, which were numerous. Someone had to steal glasses from the nearest pub, which wasn't very near as we've seen.

The Grand Vizier of parties was Colin Purbrook, one of the world's best pianists. He has what used to be called 'piano touch' which means that a skilful player can make the notes ring longer than most by holding on to some of them while laying others down: no pedals. Colin is the master of that. As a master of ceremonies it wasn't easy to forgive the overlooked details which ordained his entertainments to be disastrous. For one thing the parties were always in honour of some famous guest, usually in the music business or on its fringes. Sonny Tufts, the actor who also played drums, was one. Stan Getz was another. Neither turned up, which led cynics to believe that the invitations had been culled from an old joke: the Getz–Tufts band. But Purbrook wasn't discriminatory. *Nobody* came if the party was in his honour. Judy Garland. Coleman Hawkins. Others did come, however, but were usually told the wrong times. Kenny Graham, whose originality started the Afro-Cubists and a series of extra-polated arrangements of varying sized bands, was invited hours early on one occasion, and given a bottle of gin which he consumed before anyone else arrived at all. Later that night two girls caused a commotion by evincing alarm as Kenny, who had somehow fallen asleep in a cupboard, suddenly awoke, burst out shouting 'what's happening', clutching the empty bottle of Gordon's. Purbrook, who had by now arrived at his own party—not an invariable occurrence—took charge and confused the matter further. Thoroughly frightened, the two girls ran screaming into the night, although harm or malice were nowhere visible, and probably impossible in Fawley Road.

Some of the great musicians who lived at one time or another at Fawley Road were the pianists Brian Lemon, Colin Purbrook; sax player Tony Coe; trumpet player Jimmy Deuchar. The astonishing leaven of non-musician jazz lovers included Legal Pete, Oxford George, Ray Bolden and Al Babb. Sandy Brown and pianist Keith Ingham lived round the corner in Greencroft Gardens, and Phil Seamen, the best drummer in the U.K., in Goldhurst Terrace.

Throughout the crunch and snap of breaking glass, the splintering door panels and the endless regurgitation of overindulged stomachs (singing a rainbow), Tony Coe would flit faultlessly through Bartok or Jimmy Deuchar would write down musical figures to show what brass arranging was about. The musicians would help, correct, encourage. Bleak House was an embodiment of the archaic atelier. Centripetal forces to do with learning and extending musical frontiers were inexorably to be overcome by the centrifugal ones carried by the whirling excesses of numerous patrons of Fawley Road, but for four or five years it was a phenomenon unique in academic responsivity. It was more of a freewheel on top of power like a Saab, than an over-drive. It was like an electron accelerator: you got a push every time you came round. Everyone expected the apocalypse to be heralded by some formal dissolution, the event itself to resemble the Fall of the House of Usher in intensity: electric storms, cascading masonry, great rents appearing in walls. Far from Poe's frenzy, rents played a part. The increase was modest, but enough gradually to prorogue the unrepeatable assembly. They stole away one by one.

The park in Grange Gardens, behind the Grange Cinema in Kilburn High Road, is a typical kiddies' park. Everything has been adapted for the modern child: the child whose daylights would continue inhabiting its confident little frame through a hail of hollow threats uttered not in anger but mechanistically like a taped commercial. In such parks all serendipitous things have been found out and elimin-ated. Concrete ponds exhibit stains no magic TV abrasive can remove, and no water to help either. Water: (1) dangerous, unbreathable substance; (2) green, unpleasant (occasionally smelly) substance; (3) infectious substance: carrier of disease. Water having been removed, the NEW KIDS can get on with the relatively safe exercise of falling over the twelve-inch cliff at the edge. Resulting contusions can be remedied by the brown uniformed man with the Red Cross box and Elastoplast. Trees have lower branches lopped off. Wire netting is placed round everything. Playthings in a special compound are wrecked, removed, or kidproof-boring. The most interesting item in the park's catalogue is flat grass. This can still be dug up with determined fingers if there's been some rain. Mud and worms can be eaten. The only other hazard is cannibalism. With the limited energies at their disposal children eating each other can hardly interrupt their mothers' discussions of affairs of the day.

Like millions of other mums, shopping done, good weather would convene an informal meeting in groups of four to ten with perhaps as many as twenty children. It might be thought that for the intelligence level of the women concerned most of the talk could be classified as trivial. There would be truth in that only if one badly wrote down the words used. Facial expressions, nods, ritualistic clichés used in new contexts, lent meanings to the interchange which were nearly independent of words. At some times a competitive game would be played. The game uses all these communicative techniques and, curiously, it can be played, and won, by using anecdotal husband-lore in any form at all. It's unnecessary and sometimes even unusual for the stories to show the men's success in any sphere: finance, kudos, heroism, sexual prowess. The game could be called 'making the best of it'. This might be having a row, finding one's husband unfaithful, pissed, brilliant, a failure, rich, broke. It's also possible to break off the game in mid-stream for any reason, the children usually.

Taking a not unusual day in August 1961, five women and twelve children occupied a corner of Grange Park. Slowly, as the children spread, the talk flowed. Marion's husband 'played the string bass in a symphony orchestra': this really meant that if the L.S.O. needed eight bass players he'd have a job. If they needed seven: no. His real life was motor racing, for which he was far too old. He was extremely handsome and tall with short curly grey hair and a small beard. He'd just driven 800 miles to Stuttgart and back with his 500 c.c. racer on a trailer. The starting money was said to have paid for the trip: none of the wives understood this, nor needed to. He'd been there, raced, lost and come back. Another musician was Flo Brown's husband: he was off to Nottingham and would be in Liverpool at the weekend. He played in a band. Anne had six of the children there. She had an untroubled nature so her children's trouble threshold was high, and it always seemed as if she had double the number. Her husband was known to be writing a book, but nothing would come of asking Anne what it was about. It was also known that when the children were outrageous Anne's husband had a chain lock on his study door which was dropped in. Flo and Anne knew Edinburgh separately and Anne had known, and professed to have had some interest in, Sandy's brother, who was now a psychiatrist like Anne's husband. Quite a coincidence: two psychiatrists, two brothers: the meeting in Grange Park, Kilburn, near Mazenod Avenue where Anne and the tribe lived. Minds make patterns, sense out of nonsense—or rather sense out of nothing. (Why would there be nonsense in the first place, as if there were something deliberate about it?) If a mind was at work (and there was), why not push coincidence a little further? Anne's husband, Ronnie, was writing a book about The Divided Self—that was its title. Sandy Brown had the unreal but supplementary Al Babb. The wives had met in the park.

Little by little, vicarious introductions were made between Ronnie and Sandy: a children's party, occasional meetings. Mazenod Avenue was close to West End Lane, the nearest main route to Greencroft Gardens. Aaron Esterson, a co-author with Ronnie Laing, could be seen breakfasting on Sundays two hundred yards away in Canfield Gardens: it backed on to Greencroft. There was some interest sparked. On the one hand not too many psychiatrists at that time knew jazz musicians, particularly as 'original' as Sandy, his eclectic methods still indecipherable. On the other it was becoming clear that Ronnie Laing's approach to mental attitudes was an unusual one and this multilayeral concept seemed challengingly wrong to Sandy on two counts. Firstly the arithmetic: if you had to treat a whole family, together with friends and acquaintances, not just a disordered person, you needed more help available than seemed possible. Then the idea that schizophrenics may not simply be disordered persons, who need assistance to get back on the tracks again, but are special people with gifted insights, may be an attractive one to some but not to Sandy, whose experience certainly wasn't going to be dug out to bolster up a conceit that might reopen apprehensions about following the green plastic road again.

Antipathy was a magnet. The first real contact was an invitation to Sandy's Al Babb side to have a look at some hi-fi Ronnie Laing had installed in his study. Plainly something was wrong with it: what? The chain-lock was dropped to fend off the unruly Laing kids and a disc played. There was nothing to be done about the hi-fi. Any of it. It needed scrapping. There was a flutter on the turntable like Sidney Bechet's vibrato. The appearance was enough: the casing was inlaid wood with the kind of mid-thirties curves that came back into fashion in the late sixties with Alan Aldridge's paintings. The kind of thing you would call a wireless. However, that wasn't too much of a loss. The electronics had been bought cheaply, second-hand, and could be replaced. Some general conversation began. Sandy's brother had been a contemporary of Ronnie's at Edinburgh, and some mention of a famous previous professor of psychiatry at Edinburgh was made. Sandy thought it must be nice to have a generation-to-generation cycle like this, the sort of thing that would happen to Al Babb in architecture. No matter how different one's ideas were from the paternal generation, the framework was there. Solid and, even when ideas were totally denied, dependable. Playing jazz music from Africa with a Lowland Scots background was too big a step to allow this cosiness, or to relate to anything at all. It came back to minds making patterns out of nothing. In physics you could do this and try for a fit. Physics being an absolutely simple discipline, you could make it work quite successfully, or should it just be 'more successfully'? All the other patterns: were they there only because minds couldn't stop making them? Like the partially colour-sighted person peering at the spotty Japanese chart. The message of the barnacles on the *Rawalpindi*'s hull: a mind would make *something* of that. Do barnacles grow two miles down? Isn't that a more useful message? A question? Sandy wondered if Ronnie's idea was lean, spare enough to be no more than a 'suppose we look at what fits—however ridiculous' hypothesis like Einstein's. But, not being lovely rectilinear physics with all the imponderables tethered, the idea was too big and fat. For a start the thought was adipose with religiosity. No one would come right out and say so, but among the six or seven psychiatrists, and who knows how many others (whose tickets from the very farthest place said this on the back: 'R. D. Laing has described schizophrenia better and differently', and who consorted with Ronnie), there was a tacit rumorology, a strongly monastic mysticism, just the other side of Kierkegaard from Sartre. The word 'God', in their presence, begat equivocation.

On one occasion Sandy and the psychiatrists drank until nearly everyone had dropped. In their cups it seemed like a good idea to dispense with Al Babb and let Sandy stand unopposed. Resolve the conflicts by not needing the environment that spawns them—that sort of thing. Before the night was over, Sandy, barely anthropoid, had to be driven home, sang loudly outside his flat, woke angry neighbours, crawled upstairs, was kicked by his wife. Endgame catharsis culminating in a slight but perceptible stomach haemorrhage.

Whatever Ronnie found out about Sandy and Mr. Al Babb at the huge piss-up, it was enough. Ronnie's interest waned, and his only remaining contact with Sandy was his Ansaphone, which got itself rung up every now and then for Sandy's urgently needed hypochondriacal medication. This was for Ronnie to put Sandy in touch with the top specialist in whatever field Sandy's latest fatal disease inhabited. Miracle cures were sometimes effected in seconds. Contact was finally broken when Roger Ordish, an old friend of Sandy's, had serious arsehole trouble and Sandy asked for the top arse man on Ronnie's Ansaphone. But perhaps Ronnie had gone to Ceylon as an extension of the various communities like Kingsley Hall he lived in with mentally disturbed people. Two other contacts. Sandy met Ronnie in the club bar at the TV Centre where he was deliberating on something for a telly chat show. He introduced a young girl as somebody-or-other. 'She has become very important to me,' he said, looking closely at Sandy under his heavy-lidded eyes. So Anne had gone. Sandy still has a towelling dressing-gown she made for him. The other encounter was in *Life* magazine where Ronnie was pictured rather camply like David Lichine about to unwind into dance, wearing bare feet, half way up trees on Hampstead Heath. Who was sending up whom? If Sandy had to make a choice it would have been that Ronnie was at last conned by his own P.R. It can't have been easy, during ten years of alternative society lionization, to have held to precepts—any precepts.

Isn't it we, the Ronnie Laings and Sandy Browns, who are examined and found out; not schizophrenia, African Music, mathematics, town planning, architecture or whatever? These things are too hard. The drives that make us pursue and pontificate about them: aren't *these* under question? Aren't we flying blind without instruments? Sandy's conception was that the only really successful science is physics and that every other study demands scepticism at least, or something between that and ridicule. Suppose Ronnie Laing was completely wrong. 'It's all chemicals,' someone shouts from an X-ray crystallography room. 'Give this daft chap a shot of tcinitrotolulenase—you know, the new enzyme Nobel nearly invented: quick Watson, there's not a moment to lose. The syringe . . . there . . . how's that, old chap?' 'Pardon me, but I don't appear to have the pleasure . . . you have the advantage of me . . . er . . . how did I come to be here? Forgive me. I seem to be terribly confused, gentlemen. Good Lord. Is that the time? I must be at the Laser Reclamation Centre in Kerguelen at five.' (Little does he know he has been confined in a mental ward for two years.) 'What time does the next space tram leave?' Collapse of alternative psychiatry? Never. But we should always keep handily in reserve aphorisms for all eventualities: the more hackneyed the better.

They can be given new meanings. In the event of bio-chemical basis for schizophrenia being ascertained Ronnie can be offered, among others, the following: 'you can't win them all'.

Sandy has used this hardy device while watching Queen's Park Rangers fall out of the bottom of the First Division of the Football League with the least points in history. You can't win them all but it would have been nice to draw a few.

As the midnight train pulled wearily out of Lime Street station, one compartment enshrouded the pissed remnants of a Sandy Brown session at the Mardi Gras club. The band used to play at the Cavern, but that Liverpool landmark had long since been given over to ironclad trad and was now failing financially in preparation for the advent of the Beatles, Searchers, and all the others in the early sixties. The Mardi was run by two scouse adventurers who fortunately knew little about the internecine jazz politics of that or any other time. They were therefore persuaded to employ bands like Sandy's and Bruce Turner's, whose musical contributions were equally brigantine, if notoriously banjo-shy. To everyone's surprise, except Jim Leland (whose innocence of musical commerce made him surprise-proof), crowds of people came. They had to build a balcony to carry more crowd. From 1962 to 1966 the Mardi was one of the places to be.

The Liverpool girls were something different. There was the Jewish one who later lived as a third of Mick Mulligan's Lime Street trinity. She was the one whose duties were to run baths for Mick while the other two also had specific duties: the one who poured his drinks became a wreck through over-work. Then there was a provocative young lady with a receding chin and black hair growing in a combed line like a mane all the way down her back. I paid close attention to physical details, but seldom got close enough to examine mental qualifications, so all categories were pass level to me.

In the acetic, acid-laden atmosphere of the London train an un-flinching mental probe was nevertheless about to be applied to six drunks. Sandy produced Eysenck's Pelican IQ test book. Everyone had a turn. This established that, pissed or not, the average IQ was 125. Tony Coe helped by getting 150. Al Fairweather, however, produced a star turn. By codding about asking simpleton questions and repeating his well-known vacuous stare, the one he used on drummers, he wasted much of the time available and ended up with just under 100. From now on the vacuous stare had the backing of science. Not only could he *look* stupid and helpless: he could *prove* it.

Al had already invented a trick for dealing with musicians' inter-minable questions and aphorisms. This was to feign enough deafness to get the messages wrong. 'You can't win them all' became 'your cunt—winsome hole?' 'Yak hunt wends to mole?' 'Yukon twin thimble?' This device worked with everyone except Gay Burbidge the drummer, who later joined Chris Barber. Gay was incapable of making a statement outside of question form: 'That was a rotten blow, wasn't it?' Al allowed him twenty questions a day, which Gay used up in five minutes after getting in the band waggon, however hard he tried. After that he had to shut up for the rest of the day. In the waggon either silence or fantasy reigned. It was much deeper than a mobile dungeon. In prison the majority of captives at least had some villainy in common, or politics if it was that kind of prison. But in Sandy's bands it was seldom the case that the players had any matching ideas about music: frequently they held their colleagues' playing in a kind of resigned contempt, so either they learned quickly to bend discussions away from reality or lapsed into incommunicative apathy. The conversations were a kind of childlike game based obsessively on a single phrase or idea as a relief from the canasta board Tony Milliner the trombonist had made. Travelling through Snowdonia the remarkable scenery was pointed out to Benny Goodman the drummer. Benny's home town was the sprawling suburbia of Southend, but he looked to be winning at canasta. 'Never mind the fucking mountains,' he screamed in his squeakiest voice, 'get on with the fucking game.' A fantasy would start.

Best of order please! Now read this aloud 10 per cent faster than normal in a declamatory style: it will then sound like the British Movietone News *circa* 1938.

It seems that an acquaintance of Einstein from Berlin has arrived in Cambridge. (Pause) The German Chancellor, Herr Hitler, has begun a series of far-reaching decisions concerning the next twelve years; (pause) one of these caused Herr Schmutthausen* to come to Britain; (pause) this scientist is known to be a ladies' man, and, while charming and sexually successful in his native tongue, overstretched his tenuous command of English (pause). You can hear him speaking to his hostess, Lady Cholmondeley. Schmutthausen (bowing): 'I'm embalmed to meet you, madam. Your cunt—winsom hole.' Lady Cholmondeley (with a knowing leer): 'You're dead right, but it would be nice to draw a few.'

From the *Financial Times*: 'Yak Hunt Wends to Mole'. The international expedition to Nepal has once more been disappointed in its search for a female companion for Yki, the Regent's Park Yak.

---

* Herr Schmutthausen's body was found near the top of the Eiger. He had died of thirst. Charles McHardy, author of *The Ice Mirror*, wouldn't buy him a drink.

The trail led tortuously to 25,000 feet, where a tiny, almost blind, furry mammal was discovered in the snow. Dissent has now split the party which, if resigned to some lack of success, had certainly not bargained for continual failure.

Advertisement: It is not generally known that Eskimo garments in sealskin are sewn together using two whale bone needles simultaneously. In northern latitudes low temperatures numb senses and until recently confused Eskimos engaged in this pursuit were to be seen sitting disconsolately in igloos nursing lacerated hands. The computers of 'Blowgas Oil' of New Jersey came up with the answer. We call it 'Yukon Twin Thimble'. 'Blowgas' may not have found any oil up there—in fact we haven't found any anywhere—but we've made an improvement to the Eskimo's lot. Nowadays they're always drawing new garment patterns in the snow. Whenever they hear 'Yukon Twin Thimble' they want to draw a few.

In 1971 Sandy wrote the lyrics and music of a blues commemorating Ronnie's ideas as if the thirty-year-old episode with the anaesthetist had a straight-through trip, no hanging back, no anguish. Could schizophrenia be fun? The Big Dealer in the song is God, in whom one might as well trust as trust the rest of it. It's a gamble. Lucky Schiz and the Big Dealer:

> Sometimes I climb inside that room in my brain
> And never want to see the outside again
> I feel lucky inside
> And I know I can win
> So Dealer: Oh well well, let the game begin
>
> My room is big but I can make it real small
> Troubles on me I just pull in a wall
> I feel lucky inside
> I'm so cosy and free
> So Dealer: Oh well well, I'm so glad you invented me
>
> My eyes are open but I pulled down the blind
> No evil photons creepin' into my mind
> I feel lucky inside
> Everything there is fine
> So Dealer: Oh well well, they can't touch what is mine.
>
> You think I'm crazy but it's you that's insane
> You're runnin' scared cos you can't walk in my brain

55

I feel lucky inside
And I know I can win
So Dealer: Oh well well, let the World begin . . .

IV

It was August 1949. I'd decided to take a rest from the architectural
firm where I was an apprentice. I spent my time drawing lean-to
garages for bungalows in Edinburgh. Building licences were needed
at the time for anything over £100. You couldn't build even a lean-to
for less than about £200, but that could be fiddled by making it take
two years. Start one year, finish the next. I think you could choose
the date for the year-end yourself. The garage walls were 4½-inch
brick, except one was the wall of the house and the one at the back
had to be 9 inches thick for the first three feet in height in case you
drove the car right through everything. Corrugated asbestos roof.
Once I drew 20 in a week. They were all a little different: about
as different as the boring little bungalows they adorned.

'Why not go to Paris?' I asked Sandy. 'We went there last year.'
'Do it again: we'll get paid.' 'O.K. Set it up.' The previous year the
band had travelled to Paris on spec and had landed a job at the
Riverside Club on the Left Bank. It was small and the band got paid
by results. Two bob for each customer. It just kept us alive. I wrote to
Raymond, the owner, and asked for a three-week engagement: same
terms. Trying to do better would have taken time. The letter arrived
back in a week. Good news. The only problem was no band. Sandy
and Bugs Craig, the trombone player, could go: no one else. At that
time there weren't any jazz musicians. We got the boat anyway and
arrived at Raymond's a day late because we didn't know what to say
to him. It was worse (more embarrassing) being a day late, but I think
we wanted to forewarn him of a disaster by action (or inaction) before
having to explain about only having a clarinet and trombone. Raymond was shattered, but after half an hour on the phone he found a
trumpet player. 'Come round *now*,' he shouted into the black daffodil
on the wall. 'It's nearly two o'clock.' Ten minutes later Jean-Paul
appeared. I spoke to him in English while he sipped a Ricard. Raymond looked on anxiously. J-P was a confident little chap with good
school English. His hair was wavy and receding, an impression he
fostered by brushing it back to form a duck's arse at the back. He had
light blue eyes which jumped about slowly as if he were thinking
deeply about something: it always seemed unlikely that he was considering anything being immediately referred to him, that he'd gone

one further and was testing out an extension of whatever was the matter in hand. This impression was enhanced by the immobility of his mouth which, lips slightly parted, retained a just-about-to expression. Whether smile, speak, or distort into any of the many speechless commentaries mouths can make was never made clear. He was like a boxer. Poised. On closer study you could be sure of one thing: in no circumstances would J-P over-react.

I was discovered in my hotel room with one of his girl friends. It was visually plain that she had been sucking my cock. 'She makes that very well,' he said. His trumpet playing was awful, harmonic knowledge of the simplest nature being absent. Neither could he carry a tune very well: if in doubt, which he often was, he'd play a whole in preference to a semi-tone. This made some songs sound exceedingly bizarre. 'Alexander's Ragtime Band', for instance, started with three intervals in succession of the same whole tone. Patrons would laugh when the tune became recognizable, thinking it was a trick: a joke to catch them out. It became very wearing for Sandy and Bugs, because as soon as the semi-tones had been reinstated, at their insistence, in one tune, they'd vanish from another. It seemed as if his brain could only carry about five. Any more would overload it and semi-tones would drop out of his ears from other songs. Sandy gave up for good when a whole tone crept into 'Mood Indigo'. What J-P could do as a true professional was count people and pay the musicians (no: musicians is wrong—instrument owners) without arguments. Counting patrons was difficult because we played from eight till one or two and lots of people came in and out: some had been in before, some hadn't, and all this was counted from the bandstand. Also he'd upped our money—Raymond was too nice to run a club and went bust next year—to some impossible unmultipliable value per customer, so it wasn't hard to see where the semi-tones went.

One couldn't criticize the pianist at all, there being no musical rules which could be applied. I can more easily explain his methods by Cartesian geometry with which it had more in common. Than music it MUST have. If you take the x and y abcissa as crossing at middle C the movement of both hands were limited by $x=\pm4$, $y=8$, where inch units are used. You could have made a three-sided box, each side 8 inches, placed the open side centrally over C and started him off. His hands would thrash about inside the enclosure, usually rapping his knuckles, but not very hard, on the underside of the top. If you were to adopt these measures at home, if you have a piano and have never played before, I expect you would sound quite like this chap. There was a series of drummers, all of whom were fond of long solos, which was fine as the band got lengthy rests according to the varied but always extensive conceit of the percussionist.

The band became reasonably popular so that our finances established a kind of parity with subsistence. I was usually able to get one dance job per week to eke the money out. Bugs had discovered a vintner where red plonk could be bought for ten pence a bottle. It came out of a vat and must have been powerfully corrosive because the curved plates from which the vat was formed were like those of a thirty-year-old ship battered by heaving oceans of brine. The rivets and plate edges had blurred shapes from rust, scale, and a hundred layers of red lead.

We now stayed at the Hotel Dieppe along with *les puces*, a large variety of carnivorous insects. We would see them staggering home in the mornings so bloated with our blood that it made us squeamish to squash them. On the other hand the jumping type took a lot of squashing once caught. They had to be cracked between thumbnails or thrown into a glass of water, where, surprisingly, they sank without a struggle and lay, sometimes three deep, at the bottom, if you didn't change the water once a day.

We shared the two rooms also with other Scottish travellers who were 'passing through'. Not in any geographical sense were these Scottish itinerants passing through a place or a time, say, Paris 1949. They were passing through life, and as wayfarers rightly anticipated the customary hospitality. This endless sojourn could be weary—the ennui and despair of rootless wandering could scarcely be borne, word was somehow leaked to hosts, but it needn't be expensive. In fact it was free of charge. Occasionally among musicians, whose general generosity is infallible, one special soul would turn out to have shell-out falter. Exceptionally it would be possible to get two of these money cripples together at a bar on a night of pure magic. It could then be seen whose padlocked resolve would crack first, as pints and large scotches sank out of sight and tills flashed. This was essentially and ethnically different from the travelling Scots who have no saving sickness, no pocket paralysis. They simply have a reputation to maintain North of the Border in fiscal matters. It's a sense of responsibility that keeps them so parsimoniously skint-minded. It would only be proper to absolve those who *are* skint, but there aren't any.

One night we were playing this dance in Montparnasse. The hall was a thirtyish one, really built as a dance hall, sprung floor, revolving faceted-mirror ball and all. Everybody kept telling us about this famous Scotsman who was there. We must meet him: lived in Paris for years but still spoke poor French. His only name was 'Zhock'. The hall was crowded but we soon spotted him. No wonder. His kilt reached his ankles and his sporran was made of wood. A man I suppose in his late fifties, thick grey hair, hooked nose and jutting jaw like Punch. Not unlike Huw Wheldon. He was well known in the district, running odd errands, and was reputed to be not wholly unskilled in the decorating game. It was taken for granted that his Scottish upbringing made him reserved and introspective. So much we found from gratuitous informers. The man himself was somewhat more elusive. Every time the band got a break he disappeared. At last I caught him in a recess under the stairs. He looked trapped. ''Allo,' he said. 'What part of Scotland do you come from?' Incomprehension. 'Where are you from?' A glimmer. 'Scotland.' We crowded round and pretended animation: when we produced Bugs' tenpenny wine he joined in laughing and grunting, so we didn't give him away.

Every year 80,000 men in the U.K. go out for the papers, for a drink, take the dog out, and never come back. Where do they go? Probably the safest thing would be to go to Rome and claim to be Latvian: something like that. Where had 'Zhock' come from? Plainly he was happy in Paris. He hadn't bothered to learn either of his adopted languages and probably lived illegally; but in some overweening way it outshone his background. Martin Bormann? Hardly: *he* was escaping from more than a wedding day. Not a bad idea to treat marriage as one of these yellow cross-hatched patterns painted on cross-roads: don't enter until your exit's clear. Being a coffee colour I would first purchase a red wig, the kind of red that *couldn't* be natural, so that questions, though not ridicule, would be deterred. How much credibility would you ascribe to someone who demonstrably didn't expect his appearance to be believed? My assumed name, because I intended to live in Paris, would also be outrageous. Monsieur Jambon—made up; obviously made up and meaninglessly made-up for there was no more reason to be called Mr. Ham than for all these English names of French cigarettes immediately after the war. They were English names because they were meant to identify with English cigarettes (which could be smoked). French cigarettes were full of saltpetre and burned in half a second like a fuse, as if you had a bomb in your mouth. But the names didn't matter: they just had to be English. 'Boats', 'Bicycle', 'Hat' cigarettes. There would be a solemn picture of the article, a boat, bicycle or hat, on the packet. They fizzed and spluttered too, just as much as post-war Gauloises, so soon died out: the cigarettes and the names. M. Jambon, however, would live on foiling the Sûreté, followed from café to café but never apprehended by Maigret, as pastis and cognac were swallowed in sequence. M. Jambon would always be too small fry. The wait for the mackerel to be attracted to the impertinently counterfeit carrot-topped black sprat would be endless. My exit was clear.

At about 2 a.m. the show at the Kentucky Club started. All of us would go there. We seldom missed a night. The group of dancers, singers and musicians was from Dahomey. All the repertoire was African. Some bits of showbiz had been injected into the act. Tit and bum show was one. Then there was some rubbing of one of the male dancer's cocks—not uncovered: this was 1949—but you could see him get a hard-on and dance about with gyrating hips, staring, with white showing all round the irises, at any likely birds to explain to the audience he was symbolizing a fuck. This usually faintly embarrassed the selected girl but entertained the tourists, as much on account of the simulated violation as anything else.

When the band played for dancing the music was provided by the two small drums and one big drum. Sometimes two, other times three guitars would play. What we found so exciting about it was the steady pulse of two against three beats. It was a continuous Charleston beat, which appears on Baby Dodds's 'Rudiments'. It's the basis of all African and Afro-American rhythm. The improvisations were on top of this: either on the 2 or on the 3 pattern, or perhaps another pattern 5 or 7 could be added. Everyone knew exactly where they were all the time. None of this was original tribal music. That had already gone as the detribalization had proceeded from slavery to colonization. The missionaries had done as much harm as anyone with their simplified often simple-minded hymns. But the inner force of the rhythm was strong enough to carry the driving sophisticated beat all the way across the world and back. We were privileged to see a tiny pulse of it second-hand, and never forgot the impact.

Sandy and I would speak about it back in the room as ravenous hexopeds marshalled for breakfast parade. Sandy's feeling was one of release. This was the paradox contributed by the rigid unbreakable pulse. The contrast with the Franco–British cacophony at the Riverside must have been some relief too. 'You feel you can do *anything* with that going on.' 'Why not take some of the songs down?' 'I will, but the melody doesn't matter much. It's what you can do with *any* melody over that pulse.' 'Take them down just the same.' One of the songs was 'Dilli Mama Yey'—'Everybody Loves Saturday Night'. Sandy wrote this down with an extra passage in a minor key which he composed, and sold the song to Burlington Music (Decca's publishing house) for a tenner. 'It wasn't my song,' he reasoned, 'I just added a bit.' Sidney Bechet recorded this version and the song was a radio signature tune for Jack Jackson for over two years. All together Burlington made a thousand or two. Sandy wrote numerous songs in the same idiom but never 'sold' any more.

Back at the Riverside a girl had taken to coming every night with J-P. She brought a little square bottle of something one night and gave it to Sandy. 'What's this for?' 'La tête.' 'Comment?' 'Les cheveux.' Sandy was nearly bald at twenty. This was kind of her but Sandy's belief was that some chaps went bald and that was that. It was all chemicals again, and the ones to grow hair grew tits too. The conversation in restaurant French petered out. Her name was Pasquale. Her attachment to J-P, she hastened to tell me, was because he was a 'family friend', although why that should permit fucking wasn't explained. She spoke to me as much as she could in English and I conversed in French: there were still very long silences. She had hazel-coloured eyes which were symmetrical vertically. She had that lower lid looking much like an upper one that a few people have: like Gloria Graeme in the movies. Such eyes never open wide and the slightest movement becomes more significant than usual. She took to flicking these a fraction closer when our eyes met. I discovered that this was a sign of affection, but not by simply divining it. Not all gestures travel. I had already tried in Paris half winking an eye and quickly inclining the head to one of our regular customers, a gesture that in the U.K. means a combinatory 'all right/keep it up/look after yourself'. It meant nothing whatsoever to the Frenchman, who accepted it with a show of puzzlement and alarm. He then practised it for hours, the head inclining far too slowly and the quasi-wink hopeless uncoordinated. As I saw no point in repeating the gesture he lost touch with the original and at last the ballet became disconnected from any other voluntary movement by a normally motored person. When I used to meet him in the street a tic would start somewhere near the eyes: soon afterwards his head would slew round as if he were trying to rid his neck of a garrulous parrot, all this with the sardonic smile of the lockjaw victim. He would finish it off—a complete invention—with a military salute.

But that Pasquale's eyes meant to be friendly couldn't be in doubt when her hand closed lightly round my genitals after a few nights. Not long afterwards we were unmasked, if that's the word, by J-P opening my hotel room door as I described before. Till then I had been a very tender sexual plant indeed. Pasquale's experience was considerable, and I therefore considered it. Her husband was fighting in *that* Viet Nam war, the one that ended at Dien Bien Phu. Well, that's what she said, but I found out that she was a terrible liar. I suspected

her of having another lover—J-P had meanwhile merely adopted
another of a seemingly endless array of girls—whom she referred to as
'maman'. I was never allowed to meet her mother which could, I
suppose, have been explained by my colour, although hardly in Paris
in her class. The really odd thing was that once we turned off the
Boulevard St. Germain into her mother's street (I think it was the rue
de Rennes) I was not allowed further: maman might see us together.
I watched her once. She walked up the rue de Rennes and then turned
right into another street. She knew I had seen the manoeuvre and
plainly didn't worry about my feelings. Nor did she need to: I felt no
jealousy, nor that I owned her in any sense. Sandy asked me about
her. 'D'you love her?' What a question. I had an appetite to be
satisfied and Pasquale did that, but it went a little further. That she
showed affection for me: she bought me little things, cigarettes, a
ball-point for making notes of the figures J-P kept in his head: that
this fondness came to me from this unusual person with the flicking
eyelids seemed to evoke a flash of tenderness from me. I didn't know
whether it showed. 'D'*you* think I love her?' 'You spend a lot of time
with her.' 'She spends a lot of time with me.' 'Did she tell you she'd
swum the Channel?' 'Rubbish . . . she could be a good swimmer,
though.' I thought of her breasts which were modestly-sized but
exceptionally firm: flexed pectorals. And the seal-like eyes. 'When'd
she tell you that?' 'J-P told me.' 'Well that's second-hand for a start . . .
I don't know what love is really. I like her. She's got another geezer.'
'Yes.' 'J-P told you?' 'He said she had some soldier.' We poured out
some more tenpenny plonk. 'That's her husband: he's in Indo-
China.' 'Long way to come for a fuck.' 'Anyway when did *you* last
feel any emotion about anything?' 'Last night.' 'At the Kentucky?'
'. . . Well, not including that. Not including music.' Sandy swallowed
some more wine. 'I was going up to Finchley Road station about a
month ago. About 9.30 in the morning. There was this young chap
about 12, 13. He was running in the opposite direction for all he was
worth. He must have forgotten something for school. Running back
would make him late.' 'That's fuck all.' 'It would be to you or me, but
it wasn't to him: I saw his face.' 'So you loved him?' 'I wanted to. I
wanted to say "It's all right, it's all right", but you can't to those
people. It's never all right to them. They get burned in fires, fall over
cliffs, get cancer.' 'But you couldn't physically, sexually love those
people?' 'It's got a lot to do with it for me.' 'What are you going to do
about Pasquale?' 'Nothing.'

We left a few days later. Pasquale had offered me forty pounds to
stay. I thought it would be worse when the forty pounds was up, so I

decided to go anyway. The train was from the Gare du Nord at about
noon. We'd drunk just about as much tenpenny plonk as we could
get down and everybody was hopeless pissed. A French trombone
player with a wrecked trombone had been collected. There was a lot
of noise. Just before we were to leave Pasquale climbed out on the
window ledge and threatened to jump. It was only the first floor but
that meant about fourteen feet in the old Parisian house. She
wouldn't say goodbye. As we went down the stairs I said to Sandy:
'She might break a leg or something.' 'I don't think she'll jump . . .
but if she does break a leg it'll slow her down swimming the Channel.
Sure to . . .' We walked out of the building right underneath her.
Nothing happened. We could still hear the noise of the party. We
didn't look back.

When I returned to the architects in Leith I asked for a raise. They
wouldn't give me one and I left to go on the dole which *was* a raise. I
thought about Pasquale and the forty pounds and I didn't care what
happened: I missed her and I wouldn't pass up an opportunity like
that again.

I started out at the Main Labour Exchange at Tolcross and got
paid out by Cubby Cuthbertson who played centre forward for
Hibernian. They used to have a number of part-time players. Cubby
didn't need to be in fabulous shape. He was a poacher. Hung about
the penalty box and popped one in as often as he could. He scored an
awful lot of goals that way. Pat Patterson put me right. Pat had
joined the army to learn the clarinet, which is formidable reasoning
even for an advanced thinker. Fortunately he had stomach ulcers like
internal eczema—all tiny and curable in time—so he got out having
learned just about enough to get by. 'Stop going up to Tollcross. It's
crowded. Come down to Leith, where it's relaxing. There aren't any
jobs: you needn't worry about that.'

Pat stayed quietly on the dole in Leith till he went to Africa months
later. I joined the small queue at the same office twice a week until I
started the Art College Architecture School in October. He was right.
It *was* relaxing. Nobody went there for a job. There weren't any.
Consequently there was a pleasant, unhurried atmosphere about it
towards the end of summer. Pat and I got it fixed so we timed our
visits to coincide with opening time in one of the most famous pubs on
the Northern seacoast. This was The Jungle. I've forgotten its real
name which was innocuous. Jungle suited it best. Norwegian sailors
would burst ashore from the coasters that plied with Leith and beeline
into The Jungle which had Scotch beer and prostitutes. Ladies on the
game in Edinburgh had a lower age limit of fifty. Until I came to

c

London I thought prostitution was something you took up when you were too old for office cleaning. So it showed what a week on a coaster could do for a Norwegian.

Having time on my hands I decided to have stern words with Sandy about his future. I reminded him of the impact African music had had on him in Paris and asked him what he was going to do about this and the blues music he'd learned and the unusual clarinet technique that seemed to be coming his way. 'Tell you what,' he said, 'if you stop badgering, I'll get on with it.'

V

Bandleaders are right bastards. They steal money from their employees than whom they are very much less talented. They insist on playing repetitions and boring numbers. They hire transport you wouldn't put coal in. But their worst feature is the evil and humiliating use of lies in giving personnel the sack. The classic procedure is as follows. Imagine a cheery Christmassy scene, snow on the ground, all sounds hushed. It's four a.m. so there's not a great deal going on. Noiselessly a Ford Thames van rounds a nearby corner and stops, windscreen wipers re-arranging snow on the glass. A door opens and a figure staggers out blinking. Crump crump of neoprene soles on snow. He is holding an instrument case. 'See you, Dave,' a voice calls from inside the waggon, 'half five at Finchley Road: it's Barnet tomorrow.' Dave weaves unsteadily off. 'See you.' In the morning it seems that things could be worse. At eleven, when Dave wakes, most of the snow has gone and the sun is shining. Good time to get into the Two Brewers: have a few pints with Johnny Kendall, Ray Bolden and the Dobells lot. (Doug Dobell has specialized in jazz records in the Charing Cross Road for twenty years.) Hullo: a few letters. Two income taxes for Bill who left this address three years ago. Open the other one:

> Dear Dave, Thank you for playing in the band for two years. As a result of a change in musical policy—nothing personal— it has been decided to dispense with your services as from last night. In recognition of your services in the past it has been decided to give you a bonus of £5. As you know you had a sub of £5 on Tuesday, so that makes us even up to date. Thanks again and good luck, Dave.

Almost like a ritual Mafia killing. The victim should be replete with wine and good food before having his brains blown out. 'See you, Dave:

5.30 at Finchley Road.' That method of firing was used a lot, but bandleaders had a lot to put up with. Musicians' habits are so tiresome. They get pissed, take heroin, are extremely vague or inordinately precise—or both vague and precise like Tony Coe. In general they behave badly. Harry Brown, a trombone player, who had been known to raise a glass, worked for Laurie Gold—one bandleader who *didn't* adopt the scurrilous firing methods endemic in the profession. One night Harry turned up so pissed he had to be helped on with his white band uniform jacket. During the first number he rocked backward and forward on his heels but had difficulty in raising his trombone to his lips. It might have helped if he had used his sighting faculties to get the distance of the mouthpiece right, but these were unavailable: unfocused eyes stared out over an undulating sea of dancers. Occasionally a low rasping noise would indicate that momentary contact had been made. Laurie led him off the stage. 'Better have a seat, Harry', he said. As he returned to play with the depleted band a zombie in a white band coat followed him unsteadily on. Laurie led Harry off again. Same thing. Eventually Laurie took him off and said, 'Harry, you're fired.' As he walked back on stage he was relieved to find Harry wasn't following. Five minutes later a drunk in a white band jacket loomed through the dancers and came to rest directly in front of the bandstand. Harry rocked to and fro in this position staring gloomily at a now thoroughly unnerved Laurie for the rest of the evening.

Next morning Harry phoned Laurie up. He'd inadvertently invented a tongue-twister: 'Does this dismissal still stand?' Laurie was nonplussed.

When I heard about the 'does this dismissal still stand?' bit I saw myself standing outside the West End Café or lying on a table with a muzzle, not properly asphyxiated. Apart from being a bloody nuisance some musicians were learning my code. Sandy tried it both ways, as a bandleader and as an employee. His impression was they were both right, or both wrong.

He started a band in London with John R. T. Davies on trombone and Al Fairweather on trumpet. Al was to stay more or less for the next ten years, until he joined Acker Bilk. John R.T. had played with the old Crane River Band, a kind of New Orleans primitive facsimile, and wore a fez. No one ever found out why. He also played an alto saxophone which may or may not have been provided with an octave key: you couldn't find out by listening. This key, if depressed, raises the pitch of the note you're playing by an octave. The way John played it sounded as if the operation of the key was the result of chance

rather than deliberate choice, so it was hard to establish any meaningful melody line. Sandy had to stop him playing it. This caused a
certain amount of friction and protest in polite public school English,
which John always used, but Sandy still wouldn't allow it: it was bad
for his nerves, not because he didn't know what was coming next—
which jazz is all about—but because he could never be sure what had
just happened.

Eventually John left the band at Sandy's request. His trombone
playing had been fine, but Sandy was restless to explore some other
music and John's devotion to trad was in the way. John was a loss in
one respect: he was the kind of person you could phone up and say:
'John, I've got to get to Cairo on Tuesday, can you drive me there?'
and he'd be over in ten minutes. Never needed an explanation for that
kind of thing. But neither Sandy nor I ever wanted to go to Cairo in
haste. John needed that kind of environment, and found it in the
Temperance Seven, who *all* seemed to be frantically *en route* to
Mandalay or some other suitably John R.T. place.

What Sandy's band never had was a policy. It had no objectives.
No star was to be hitched to. No advice was given to new musicians.
In one or two cases musicians were discouraged from pursuing one
course or another in the realm of timing. Sandy, in a sub-expressive
form, felt rhythms almost like an intrinsic and immutable alphabet:
his own playing, which so contemptuously dismissed the positioning
of notes, depended utterly on a steady pulse. Without it he was sunk—
often. No other constraints were placed.

At the height of the trad boom it might have been easy to follow
the bonanza or it might have been difficult. Many tried. At one time,
in 1960, there were sixty professional trad bands more or less on the
road. Only half a dozen made the kind of living a junior planning
officer for Fenny Stratford could expect, although the aims, methods,
and to some extent musicians, were indistinguishable. One band from
Glasgow was called the Clyde Valley Stompers. Their original leader
admired and emulated the methods of Chris Barber, whose band had
evolved as a breakaway from Ken Colyer's New Orleans fanaticism.
The personnel of the band changed from week to week as there was no
personal imprint, and it didn't matter who turned up so long as an
impostoral Barber band sound was available.

One night I met them playing in Hull. Sandy and I knew most of
the chaps from Scotland: the following week we met them in Liverpool. Different chaps. 'See you next week,' they'd said, but you know
about firing methods. In the interim no member of the band was left
undischarged, some were sacked, many left. A typical itinerary for

this band's week was Bristol, Glasgow, Dover, Aberdeen, Penzance, London, Edinburgh: so they lived in the waggon. They had a unique way of retaining sanity: about every three days they would stop the waggon, go into a field and punch each other senseless. By an evolutionary mechanism that requires more study than I can afford, some fine musicians came out of the band. Perhaps it was just that so many played in it over a period of five years. Closely typed, the surnames would have covered ten pages of A4. But the best one was Forrie Cairns, a clarinettist who gave Sandy cause for concern on the occasions they occupied the same bandstand. Forrie's playing was a fierce amalgam of a number of New Orleans originals, notably Ed Hall, but derivative or not it had a grating perseverance that outlived the interminable punch-ups and changes in personnel. Sandy had always assumed he had the edge on any clarinettist in Europe, and Forrie made him more uncomfortable than anyone except Tony Coe. Given the freewheeling, uncommitted atmosphere of Sandy's band Forrie could have been unbeatable: he was never provided that climate, and was consequently under-rated. Everything went by precedent. If a band had become successful it was copied until the sterility of its methods concreted. I was guilty of this too—was it guilt? I insisted that Sandy's band play the African numbers Sandy had written: 'African Queen', 'Africa Blues', 'Everybody Loves Saturday Night', 'Go Ghana'. These had become popular with the trad crowds and one of them—I forget which—made what was then called the hit parade and was number one in Denmark. As this was pre-1960 and the population of Denmark is 5 million it didn't mean very much financially, but this and the other African songs kept the band on the road in reasonable financial shape between 1956 and 1966.

The band hated playing these numbers so Sandy and Al Fair-weather wrote many others which were recorded but were never played again. Other bands found this difficult to believe and fans, who had bothered to buy the records, were disappointed and angry when 'Ognaliya' (Ayilango, from Sanders of the River), 'Scales' and dozens of others never got played. I felt we were on a green record slowly revolving into pink jaws and requests were politely refused. There was no conscious effort to find out what jazz was about or what the effects of a band policy would have been, but the feeling of being trapped once again was strong. The buzzing noise was nearer and the sweating crowds seemed to be cracking down on us through the acrid armpit stench, pushing us back into the room in our heads. Perhaps we should have punched each other to pieces in a field under the stars twice a week, but we weren't that kind of people. This might have made it easier to play the same shit every night like everyone else, but we couldn't.

I did a deal with Lyn Dutton. He ran sixteen bands on the road including Humph Lyttelton and Chris Barber. We got their cast-offs. As Humph had been to Eton, acted it, and Chris Barber's band made more money than the other fifteen bands for the agency, both could demand comfortable itineraries, so even their discards were about a thousand miles a week short of the headlong thrash of the Clyde Valley's roller-coaster. Some time to think with. Sandy wrote some songs: Al wrote songs and arrangements; the band began to attract some attention from those who detected a flaw in the 'pure' jazz arguments. This gave the impression of originality, but Sandy's method was a fragmentation and rearrangement of existing disparate rubrics. If a gestalt ever came his way it sailed right on into oblivion: his creed had no machinery to receive or even recognize one. Through time he graduated from the view that few musicians were gifted with absolute invention to the reassuring knowledge that none were. This kind of B. F. Skinnerism relieved him from fruitlessly scratching about in search of his own musical persona and allowed him to steal from sources with 'good' and 'bad' labels indiscriminately, like he believed all the great musicians had done before. Louis Armstrong would take a phrase by King Oliver and alter its structure. A typical case would be the last two bars of a song leading up to another chorus:

Where Armstrong got the triplets from might be Africa or a Viennese waltz, but the exciting transformation is at the end of bar one, where he anticipates the resolution on the C chord by playing the keynote as the second two-thirds of a triplet and leaving it before the resolution arrives.

Armstrong acknowledged his debt to Oliver. He also claimed, all his life, that one of his major influences had been Guy Lombardo's band. This was a white 'sweet' band, with undistinguished arrangements always apparently dating from a period ten years earlier than the performance, but with accurate section work and strict tempos: a ballroom dance band. Most of Armstrong's admirers flatly refused to believe his admiration of such a pedestrian model. They could find no trace of Lombardo in his playing. Nor could Sandy, but he believed the debt was real. It was one of Armstrong's strengths that he ignored intangible qualities like 'taste' and pursued a perceptive eclecticism better than any other musician of his era.

Similarly, when Lester Young listed Frankie Trumbauer as one of the major influences who helped him to revolutionize sax playing in the late thirties, his followers put it down to erratic behaviour resulting from over-indulgence of one sort or another—Lester neither smoked nor drank till his early twenties, but he quickly and thoroughly made up lost ground until his death in 1959. Sandy saw no reason why Trumbauer shouldn't have been a big influence on Lester. Outwardly, Trumbauer's style was an extension of the staccato almost vibratoless white school started by Rudy Wiedtoft (after whom Rudy Vallee was nicknamed), but Lester certainly heard a lot of Trumbauer who was an almost unavoidable companion of Bix Beiderbecke's recording career. And, somewhere in the depth of Trumbauer's tone, cool jazz was born: that we know about it is due to Lester's honesty and gratitude. As a species, and necessarily confining the subject to music, musicians are open-heartedly dead honest. You can safely take anything they say on the subject absolutely at face value. Straying into other fields, acceptance of any views they care to express would be disastrous. That some of their irrational views on every aspect of human behaviour is due to an apprenticeship served between walls of tin, hurtling through nowhere, five hours a day, over a period of years, is unquestionable. Every member of every touring band (and that means every jazz musician because none escaped a period of waggon-pressure) bears mental scars which never heal.

Everything became hurried even when there was plenty of time. Touring Denmark with Sandy was a microcosm. At the port of Esbjerg—it was too expensive to travel by plane—the band was met by Bent, the tour manager or 'roadie' set up by the Danish agency. He was a garrulous young chap in his twenties with a good command of forties Hollywood English and an inexhaustible bumper-fun library

in his head. 'Say you fellas, did you ever hear ze one about ze English-
maan and ze Jewish fella?' would wring a spontaneous burst of
merriment designed to prevent hearing any more of the insufferable
howler. This puzzled and saddened Bent, as did the band's determined
strides in any direction from railway stations, leaving luggage on the
platform. 'Where you going fellas?' A hint of eye-panic. 'Hotel.' 'But
iz wrong direction.' This device avoided waiting for Bent to phone for
a microbus thereby saving the cost of two taxis. On such occasions
non-musicians were treated as pets, not humans. Long-term satisfactory behaviour could be secured quickly without explanation by
adopting simple and cruel training methods appropriate to animals.
How could pets understand motives? Just do what's required and you
won't be in trouble. Teach them a lesson. They weren't animals of
course, and Bent quickly learned his joke-book was out of date, that
two taxis were needed everywhere and that any further display of
eye-panic would encourage a new, less bearable torture. As the Brown
band drank, retched and fucked its way through Jutland Funen and
Zealand he withdrew from avoidable contact. On the last day again at
Esbjerg he stole away without a farewell. Nobody cared, and his
antics, the results only of having miserly employers and an im-
perfected accent, were enlarged upon and mimicked for months in the
band waggon.

On this tour the pianist was Stan Greig who claimed some relationship with Greig, the Norwegian composer. Latterly, just before he
joined Acker Bilk, we thought he must have been the composer's
uncle. His attitude to any situation was avuncular. Stan was a fine
pianist and drummer: we carried two sets of drums at the time, so that
Gay Burbige and he could finish the show with a whoop-up. It never
failed. Stan ran the rhythm section, as all Sandy's pianists did. This
responsibility was more onerous than in some bands because the
personnel kept changing. There wasn't a drummer you could name
who didn't play with the band at one time or another, and I phoned
up 25 brass players one Saturday without success for a dep.
Eventually I tried Jack Fallon once again. His list of deps was more
comprehensive than Whitaker's Almanac and contained names
the Musicians' Union had never heard of. 'Listen, Alastair,' he said,
'there's one guy who I know *for sure* isn't working tonight.' 'Why?'
'Because he's at the bottom of my list.' Sure enough, the bottom-of-
the-list man turned up, a man who had played with Humph Lyttelton
in his early days. He looked as if he'd slept in his suit. 'Lucky guess',
he said when this was put to him: everyone read the same comic
books in waggons. The band started with a medium-slow tempo

12-bar blues in B flat. At the end he looked near collapse. 'Fuck me,' he croaked, 'I hope you're not going to keep *this* up all night.' But most of the deps could play very well: difficulties still arose with arrangements, and as Sandy refused to have anything to do with deps it was all down to the pianist. Stan, Colin Purbrook and Brian Lemon shared this over the years, along with Barney Bates and one or two others for shorter periods.

Sandy's retreat from this aspect of bandleading came the first night drummer Dave Smallman played with the band. Eel Pie Island, a muddy eyot on the Thames, supported a decaying Adam family residence simply called 'Hotel'. Dave arrived at the riverside with naked drums: no cases. At that time an unreliable chain ferry hauled visitors across the few yards of water. A bridge was built later. The band started playing to a few customers. No mention was made of Dave's habit of dropping bombs during these introductory noises: he was a bopper and you don't change boppers. One of the songs in the repertoire was Neal Hefti's 'The Midgets', which was played somewhat faster than Basie's version to give Tony Milliner a chance to show off his agile technique on trombone. Sandy turned to Dave: 'Give us four in,' he said, 'about as fast as you feel comfortable.' Smallman took this to be a crucial challenge and thundered off at the speed of light. The four bars disappeared before anyone had time to get instruments to their mouths. At the end of the first eight nobody was within a bar of each other, and Sandy, whose maximum speed demanded a half tempo approach above a certain velocity, was already committed. In these situations he would stare straight ahead in riveted panic and slur through pieces without tonguing at all so no one knew where he was.

As Smallman careered on, the front line flared into action from time to time, briefly, like exhausted fireflies. After about five minutes he suddenly stopped, having presumably reached an even multiple of sixteen bars (at three bars per second: 360 beats a minute). No word was spoken. A look was exchanged. The look had a name. It was the 'who's your friend?' all-purpose look. For reasons that will become clear, you can't examine this look in a mirror: you will need an observant friend to describe it for you. Firstly, face your friend; next, grit your teeth hard enough to force perceptible strain on—and a slight tremor if possible of—the lips, which should be just failing to smile. If you can persuade a vein to stand out (like Conrad Veight always did when his U-boat was sinking) so much the better. Now the vital final ingredient: de-focus your eyes so that you can see two of your friend, both blurred. This produces a calmness beyond stress and terror: it's the ultimate calmness of someone who has come to terms with unimaginable misfortunes. Years later I asked Sandy about drummers. Why did he leave so much up to them? Everyone knew they were idiots.

VI

Sandy's reply on drummers

Why pick on drummers? Why not bass players? Or tenor players? You could then cite Ron Mathewson or Tony Coe, write a paper on it, and get a bust of yourself in the Royal Society beside Faraday. Dave Smallman turned up with bare drums, right? Who was the other nude drummer: no covers? Danny Craig of course. Dan didn't even have whole skins on his bongoes. He was anything but supersonic. There's no pattern. You could say they all died young: and they did. But there was no pattern. Six of the drummers in my bands died in six years. The obvious rejoinder is 'no wonder', but they took some tragic ways out for guys collectively gifted with so much talent. I didn't use Dave Smallman very often and the only event that really sticks in my mind was 'The Midgets' disaster. That was my fault. I should have kicked it off, I suppose. I bore him no malice. It was kind of useful to know I couldn't play at 360 beats a minute using half notes. Tonguing 12 notes a second is beyond me: I'm grateful to Dave for bringing it home so practically. I certainly wouldn't have raised my hand to him, although he was a bit like his name—small. Someone did, though. Dave Smallman was murdered.

When they found him he was naked and trussed up with wire or flex or something. He'd been dumped on a bomb site. No one ever found out why. Nor did they find who did it. The police had some kind of lead, which I've forgotten, but none of the band was questioned: we didn't have to play 'The Midgets' either, thank goodness: it had been quietly dropped from the repertoire into the ooze of Eel Pie Island. Dave hadn't played with us for over a year before his executioners caught up with him.

I never discovered how Benny Goodman died. Al Fairweather told me about it many months after the event. Benny had played with the band for about eighteen months three or four years previously. I can't say I, or anyone else in the band, ever got round to liking him, but he had two skills which were remarkable—one was unique: he could play in 3/4, 6/8, 12/4 or any 3-based time signature and make it sound as if it were a 4-based beat. I never heard any other drummer do this or even approach it. When Benny was in the band we had a number of arrangements in 3-based time and almost unbeatable soloists in Tony Coe, Tony Milliner, Al Fairweather and either Colin Purbrook or Brian Lemon on piano. The effect on other musicians was quite shattering. In other ways Benny was sometimes a very ordinary drummer and as a personality quite disgraceful—except to children, whom he genuinely liked and who, to my amazement, instantly took to this undersized young bald chap with an aggressive and truculent manner.

It was a complete waste of time employing logical or even sequential thought in discussion with Ben, so nobody did. He would take meaningless rambling solos which varied in tempo (which is itself acceptable of course) but had no perceptible form. 'Ben,' I said, 'how are we supposed to know when to come in?' Ben looked aggrieved. 'Will . . . I do moi bit and ven you come in wiv yors.' 'When?' 'Wen I'm finished.' 'How can we tell?' There would then follow a discourse on expression of feeling through musical instruments which could have been scripted by a guide for day trips down the Alph. On safe arrival at the sunless sea I would say, as usual: 'You can have two choruses Ben. We'll treat it as in tempo and count like mad.' It was a point of honour to count accurately for two choruses and come in on the button. It was terribly difficult to do, of course, because Benny's tempo shifts immediately prevented his contribution from sounding like a drum solo: more like someone shifting furniture. Then he was never ready to come in when the band hit the next chorus, so the band had to hold the tempo for about six to eight bars rigidly so Benny could get in gear.

Near Loch Garten in the Rothiemurchus Forest north of the Cairngorm mountains the osprey nests. This it does on the very crown of a Scotch pine, that unkempt fir with all its patchy foliage at the top as if struck by a form of floral alopecia. While one of the parents fishes in the lake the other sits motionless on the nest with its head looking over its left shoulder. At ten-minute intervals its head will jerk into the straight ahead position. Benny Goodman never saw an osprey but his physical appearance at the drums was indistinguishable from the one-move tableaux I've described, even to the aquiline hebraic nose.

Come to think of it, Benny's movements increasingly inclined towards immobility—it couldn't be called repose: the tension could be measured in zillions of Newtons per angstrom unit. 'A Newton is about the same weight as an apple, Ben, that's why it's called that. And an Angstrom unit is the maximum diameter you can let your arsehole open after three chicken vindaloos when remote from

73

sewage disposal.' Benny's sticks would encounter each other in flight from one part of the kit to another and would lodge there, crossed and stuck, in mid-air. Ben's hands could only push them together. A non-return mechanism. This was quickly detected off-stage where the rest of the band were pissing up, or smoking. While the bass drum pedal boomed on everything else had stopped with Benny's seizure. We would run round to get a good laugh. Mercy was rightly considered a dangerous perversion in the band waggon. At last some dis-equilibrium would allow one stick to slide past the other and Benny's indecipherable nonsense would continue replete with crashing cym-bals, snare and tom-toms. All this time we would be counting, and would suddenly start playing whenever an agreed even number of choruses had elapsed. It still never failed to surprise Benny. Always the wrong moment as far as he was concerned. His reserves of naiveté were quite limitless: that the band came, always, together on the same beat, he was willing to accept as a perpetual coincidence.

Discovery of this fat seam of gullibility led to totally absurd inventions being fed to Benny. After a dismal night in separate Brighton boarding houses, Brian Prudence, the bass player, and I, who had shared the worst one, launched into a description of sexual delights showered on us by the lady of the house and her daughter. The intrinsic geometry of parts of the story aroused, for once, Ben's suspicions. On being informed of the ladies' previous employment as 'Bertram Mills's Indiarubber Ladies' all doubts were assuaged, and we then had enormous difficulty conjuring up new, and worthy, variants.

Ben should have had the last laugh. His real name was David: 'Benny' was one of those nicknames given at early ages for showing an interest in something. One day a young girl researcher from the B.B.C. rang up. Benny Goodman the clarinettist was in London and a TV interview was being set up. 'Mr. Benny Goodman?' 'Yais.' Benny's accent was yodelling cockney though he came from Southend. 'I wonder if you would like to be interviewed on TV about your work in jazz . . .' and so on. 'Will . . . wasse money loike?' 'Oh, it's not a great deal I'm afraid. £50 plus expenses, but of course it will help to publicize your performances.' 'To hell with publicizing performances,' thought Ben, 'fifty nicker: fucking marvellous.' 'Roight. Where do I have to be?' The arrangements went on for some weeks, but a cog in the Beeb cottoned on to the Bow Road Kosher accent—which Ben to his credit never tried to conceal—and it was all off. Ben got paid some-thing for the cock-up, but it would have been nice to hear his life story in jazz from the wrong B.G. The one with the osprey's posture, sticks glued together, seated at the drum kit slowly moving down the spiral green ramp with the pink walls. One thing certainly: looking over his left shoulder he couldn't have the gaping maw before or behind him.

Soon after Ben left the band he was accompanying Dexter Gordon at Ronnie Scott's Old Place in Gerrard Street. Tony Milliner went to see him there and caught the end of the show, after which Dexter, at 6 ft. 4 in. towering over Benny's 5 ft. 0 in., was making some complaint or other. Waste of time: Benny just shrugged his shoulders. Dexter would have to learn to count.

Dan Craig, from Dundee, liked a drink. It showed in his drum set. There were no skins on the undersides because each unit had to double as a drum and a receptacle for spirits. His drumming, let it be said, was excellent. At his very best, which I suppose was around 1960, I played in the Studio Club with Percy Heath of the M.J.Q., Alan Clane on piano and Dan on drums. I've played with a great many rhythm sections. That was close to being the best. With a good section your freedom is boundless. Even without one, if you're good enough, you can put the beat almost anywhere and maintain tension. Louis Armstrong's 'Potato Head Blues' and 'Tight Like That' are examples of invention beyond the need of outside rhythmic aid. Coltrane used clusters of five notes in a four-time setting (or at least *even* time setting) but there's something else you can do with a good beat laid out for you: it's this. If you're careful where you place the note, you can be non-committal. That turns the option over to the listener as to the way he wants to hear a piece. How he wants to hear exactly the same recorded version of the piece. I'm talking about a listener already committed to thematic listening methods.

- 3 -

Contributions to 'The Listener' 1968-73

6 June 1968

ONTOLOGICALLY UPTIGHT

I was playing the clarinet in this shoe factory near Bawtry. The happening was like a televised *Workers' Playtime*: non-stop music. The arranger had it fixed so that, however, remote bar lines were, the last note of a melody was immediately succeeded on the next beat by the first note of another song. Didn't want to waste time, you see. Most tunes are fabricated from eight-bar measures and while some have a run-up like 'I'll Never Smile Again' others, like Tchaikovsky's *Pathétique* theme (the one known in Denmark Street as 'The Story of a Starry Night'), start on the second beat of the first bar. Some unusual time-signatures were generated by the baton changes. When I saw a farthing winging along the manuscript I panicked.

If the bar of one/four exposed my musical illiteracy it was still, I thought, a poor way of explaining something simple and banal. I was reminded of this humiliating episode by the accelerando of the Keller–Mann–Mellors–Cooke toady-in over the Lennon–McCartney songs. Picking one of the least original examples, Deryck Cooke in the *Listener* ascribed to 'Yesterday' a subtlety largely to do with the omission of the final bar of the *a* segments in the conventional pop song's *a a b a* format. What Lennon and McCartney had done was to miss out the instrumental fill-in. As soon as the lyric ended, they started the next stanza without waiting for the music to catch up— a trick learned from the archaic Blues singers. Formally it was indistinguishable from the shoe factory sing-along.

Ontologically uptight, Cooke presumed a preposterous prescience in explaining that the melody was distributed mutually so that one phrase could do the work of two. This explanation doesn't work at the entry to the middle eight bars, by the way. Lucky for him that pop wasn't OK scholars' grist when Monty Sunshine's 'Petite Fleur' was number one some years ago, or he might have committed himself to a paragraph or two about the mysterious loss of occasional half bars which were cut out of the tape in error. The trouble is that most pop

76

music is not amenable to investigation by the scholastic tools that are being used. In one sense the magnification is too great: graininess becomes a meaningful field of particles. In another it's too insensitive: some sort of musico-literary electron beam would be needed to illuminate what was wrong with Bobby Gentry's brave attempt at the blues form in 'Ode to Billy Joe' and what's right about Aretha Franklin.

Getting back to form: there's a big difference between truncating or expanding melody lines to fit round lyrics and deliberately introducing

maverick bars or time-signatures in the way that the Bacharach–David songs do. The latest Dionne Warwick vehicle, 'Do you know the way to San José?', is typical, and as good as any. Some lip service is paid to the *a a b a* form but *a* equals five bars, *b* equals 20, and the instrumental and choral backings together with the first two bars of the five-bar *a* portion are multiples of two or four.

At a time when, as I seem to have said, unreasonably erudite discussion of pop songs is burgeoning, jazz musicians have become more conservative in their choice of basic pop as improvisatory material. Their repertoire is the Gershwin–Porter–Rodgers–Arlen song book (all of which, incidentally, you can hear on record sung rather well by Ella Fitzgerald with various backings, all good). Even recent additions ('Here's That Rainy Day', 'When Sunny Gets Blue', 'Misty') are paradigmatic. 'Misty' is the work of Erroll Garner, a jazz musician; and Marvin Fisher, whose dad used to write songs for Al Jolson, was sufficiently influenced in 'When Sunny Gets Blue' to include a slow-motion Charlie Parker invention in the second and third bars of the melody.

Modern pop songs don't suit the improvising habits of jazz musicians. There just aren't enough harmonic changes per mile, and the ones that do occur are so determinedly triadic that the kind of extension jazz players insist on would destroy the character of the piece. One result is that there is now a widening formal gap between pop and jazz. I find this sad because shedding public involvement always seems to herald the adoption of a course perilously close to the antics of the oozalem bird; and I'm not so daft as to imagine that it's only a matter of time before the butchers' boys' lips purse in anticipation of a programme of Stockhausen and Albert Ayler.

Meanwhile a more cheerful consequence is the substantial increase in original composition by the younger British jazz musicians. Christopher Gunning, Richard Hewson and the prolific Graham Collier have all had some highly original work performed recently, mainly at Ronnie Scott's Old Place, which tragically closed last week owing to troubles with the lease. Of the three, I am least familiar with Gunning, whose compositions I have played in public rather badly on a number of occasions. But I find him impressive. He writes with a youthful arrogance, though avoiding rhetoric. We shall hear more of him: the question is where? The Old Place is gone and the projected London Jazz Centre is as yet no more than a dream.* A glimmer of photons is escaping from the Arts Council, who seem, at last, to have recognised the idiom and the need. The Jazz Centre project is to be one of their

* Now at last to be realised as the National Jazz centre in Floral Street, Covent Garden. *Ed.*

beneficiaries if it gets off the ground. If this does no more than establish the principle of public patronage for jazz, it can't be bad.

5 December 1968

AT THE RABBI'S GRAVE

The exposition of jazz music is evidently considered too important to be left to musicians. The annual festival trail—the golden road to Berlin via the Odeon, Hammersmith, Ronnie Scott's, Prague, Vienna and Warsaw—was abrupted by Russian tanks in August. Hands subsequently played by the Politburo, the State Department and other political agencies destroyed the programme arrangements for some of the European jazz festivals this year. Western countries were scarcely affected but the Prague festival was held almost clandestinely two months late, with all the Warsaw Pact musicians excluded, and was hampered by native defection. Warsaw was forbidden by the State Department, boycotted by Czechs, and grumbled about nebulously by the Foreign Office. The net result, for those who penetrated the nets, was a warming reassurance that this music is virile enough to overcome most kinds of planned idiocy. Western musicians who turned up in Warsaw included Cecil Taylor, Memphis Slim, Beryl Bryden and me. A half-forgotten addition was Hal Singer, who plays tenor sax as convincingly now as he did with numerous bands from Lucky Millinder in. Just to hear this unfashionable man's huge tone swinging the audience by the scruff was a mutual joy. Memphis Slim was a little too beautifully restrained. He couldn't be persuaded to sing his 'If you see Kay'—a lovely précis of the blues-hearted lyrical innuendo which is still the only effective anti-coagulant in American taboo, but a marvellously decorated 'Every Day' made me wonder again why Joe Williams's version with Basie was the one that caught on. Cecil Taylor thrashed about the piano meaningfully for ten minutes, repetitively for 30, and England's Queen of the Washboard, Beryl Bryden, brought the house down aided by a clock-work Dixie band.

Okayed by Western governments, the Prague festival enjoyed a substantial dollar bonus in the form of the Illinois State University Jazz Band, a wholly owned subsidiary of the State Department. The aging personnel reminded me of all those films about university life where the professors appear younger than the undergraduate stars. It's a fine band and would have outshone the Gustav Brom professionals from Brno if trumpeter Maynard Ferguson hadn't been fronting for Brom.

Of all the recruits to the Eastern European festivals this autumn the oddest man out was unquestionably Tony Scott, who was concerned peripherally with the Charlie Parker movement in the Forties. No two critics or musicians have been able to agree about his contribution to jazz, opinions varying from admiration to contempt. Visually, his performance in Prague was grotesque. Pecking like a demented chicken jack-knifing every bar, his shaved head bobbed alarmingly at the thin end of a clarinet whose bell described an arc only a few degrees short of a full circle. But if he played in a splint, his sound would be eccentricity enough. His shrill tone must be the loudest in the world. I played with him for hours into a drizzly Prague morning and came away with the exhilarating feeling that breaking all the rules had worked. The sensation lasted well into the following day when I was arrested for breaking some rules I hadn't thought of.

The technical standard of the state-trained Eastern European jazz players was very high. I couldn't think of much else to say about them until I discovered one day that a possible model for the Frankenstein story is buried in the Jewish cemetery in Prague. It seems the Rabbi Levi made a man of clay in the 16th century. He activated his dummy by putting a magic word in its mouth. I expect you know the rest: the Rabbi's assistant got the word wrong and awful things happened. We're all clay men in Europe and if you're at the end of a bad connection you're likely to get the wrong word. The Rabbi's grave is covered with stones representing, I'm told, the fulfilled wishes of the donors. If I could have perched one more without starting an avalanche, I would have wished to erase cultural frontiers and put an end to a tragic blockade of talent.

6 February 1969

AT THE MALTINGS

Benjamin Britten's Aldeburgh Festival Hall is one of the best bargains in the history of musical architecture. Respectfully converted from the old maltings at Snape—the naked brickwork glows a cosy red with pride—the hall seats 800 souls, a term no secularist would shun, standing in the no man's land between earth and ocean that borders Snape. It's always a surprise, here, to travel eastwards, knowing that the countryside has given up to the sea, and come across a town as big as Aldeburgh only a few hundred yards from the ships cutting the corner at England's North Sea salient.

Someone has the bright idea of televising a series of jazz concerts at

Snape for BBC-2. The programmes, *Jazz at the Maltings*, are directed
in his usual free-wheeling style by Terry Henebery. Unlike most TV
jazz, the sound is good—something of a triumph, as the hall's live
acoustics don't make it easy to strike a balance with a lot of percussion
about. The problems were emphasised in the first show, which featured
drummer Buddy Rich's band. Displaying commendable opportunism,
the BBC filmed a bland *ciné vérité* record of the band's arrival and
rehearsal. The result shown on *Late Night Line-Up* was a hilariously
gripping description of one of the worst days in Henebery's life. Rich
is an irascible fellow, and the four-hour car ride had almost, it
appeared, unhinged him. He stumbled out of the limousine, looking
like Lee Marvin in one of his most misanthropic roles, and said
menacingly to Henebery: 'Are you responsible for this?' I thought he
was going to smash him in the face. Musicians wandered dreamily
round the building. Snatches of incredulous unaddressed questions
were heard. 'A TV studio in a *swamp?*' 'Do they have real estate out
here?' Rehearsals without an audience exaggerate the hall's reverbera-
tion and BBC minds turned to thoughts of the small print on the
contract when Rich threatened to cancel the show. It was all right on
the night, however, by which time Rich had cooled sufficiently to
apply his fiery temperament to proving that he's still the most
spectacular big-band drummer in the business.

The rest of the series comprised music by almost every available
top-ranking jazz player and the tapes are now safely in the archives,
stored for the future wonderment of BBC-1 viewers. A performance by
the Oscar Peterson Trio was broadcast on 23 January. Peterson stands
at the end of a long and honourable tradition of jazz piano playing
originally known as 'Harlem stride'. The stride refers to a left-hand
vamping method using alternating tenths and note clusters at least an
octave apart. Sometimes the tenths are repeated, so that they
exchange beats with the clusters: oom-ching-oom-oom ching-oom-
oom-ching, giving a hair-raising eccentricity to the rhythm. If it's to
be any good at all, the vamp must be perfectly regular and the
progressions accurate. This is difficult to achieve at speed. Not many
normally proportioned left hands can stretch a tenth with the pinky
on a black note. Try it. Mastery of the vamp is no more than a
season-ticket to the tradition; the use of it is almost peripheral. You
will recognise that kind of thrown-away expertise as the hallmark of
an exclusive club, which Harlem stride was.

Shortly before his death, Lucky Roberts told me that when Jelly
Roll Morton arrived in New York in the late Twenties as the 'inventor
of jazz' and played his compositions to the Harlem team, eyebrows

81

were raised no further than the pejorative 'don't ring *us*' level. It's not hard to believe on the evidence. The technical equipment of Harlem pianists was superb. The stride pianist's right hand is free-ranging and uses fast brilliant runs and note clusters borrowed from ragtime and machine-cut piano rolls. Early masters of the style were Lucky Roberts, James P. Johnson and Willie the Lion. The tradition was nobly carried on by Fats Waller and came to a dazzling peak in the hands of Art Tatum, the most astonishing virtuoso in jazz. Tatum largely dispensed with the vamp, although he was a complete master of it, replacing it with a fantasy of two-handed harmonic runs and clusters of his own invention. His break-neck tempos were so staggering that, to some ears, they overshadowed his prodigious gifts in the field of chromatic harmony. A number of subsequent pianists, notably Phineas Newborn, managed to recapture some aspects of Tatum's style while adding fragments from later experimenters like Bud Powell. No one except Peterson reproduced the relentless down-home swing that underlay the decoration.

Peterson came from Montreal, far outside the home ground of the Harlem men where techniques could be studied first-hand, and he set himself terrifying disciplines to catch up. Pianist Brian Lemon, Peterson's apostle in Britain, tells this story: Peterson claimed that he could fit into a given harmonic sequence any separately given root note. He demonstrated this by having Lemon shout random roots at him while he improvised on a standard sequence. The roots were incorporated without rhythmic interruption. Apart from the flamboyance of this gesture, which I enjoy—it's the kind of thing that persuades me to watch Rodney Marsh of Queen's Park Rangers every fortnight—it strips the argument from Peterson's critics, who think a well-programmed computer could do his thing. Fitting random notes to established harmonies could only be engineered by knowing, intuitively, which liberties could be taken using chromatically altered chords. This is exactly what computers aren't about.

At the Maltings, Peterson rested his left hand for a few passages, intensifying the accuracy and swing of his right. I suppose you might say this was showing off. I don't care if it was—it made for beautiful listening and tuition. J. S. Bach wasn't bad at this. Virtuosity lives!

31 July 1969
MYTH AND HINDEMITH

The chiels that winna ding (yield), according to Robert Burns, are facts. I'd go along with that in the long run, and the run from Wagner to Archie Shepp should be long enough to test the strength of Burns's assertion if there's a fact still dinging. There *is*: resonance. Every musical scale is built in a hierarchical way on the physical phenomena of resonance, the prime relationship being the octave, the next the fifth (which becomes the fourth when inverted), then the third, and so on. Paul Hindemith, in one of his books on harmony, explains all this pretty well, together with the inevitable complexities that Bach had to tinker with to allow varying tonalities. Schoenberg kept the 12 notes we ended up with but threw the hierarchy out the window. As no acoustic environment is entirely free from harmonic distortion— resonance again—Schoenberg was literally flying in the face of nature. The often quoted visual analogues are spurious: no animal can *see* a complete octave in electromagnetic terms (light), so resonances are invisible. All can *hear* a wide enough range—most, including people, encompass nine octaves—to make acoustic resonance undingworthy. When you get to tee on the solfeggio scale, however, far from being Oscar Hammerstein's drink with bread and jam, so many physical compromises have had to be made for Wagnerian harmony to work that everything becomes dubious if you suddenly decide to make tee a new doh. Jazz musicians came to this problem late, 50 years after Schoenberg had humourlessly chosen to invent a system which his performers didn't understand and their instruments still can't (because instruments have their own immutable resonant hierarchy). Jazz is none the worse for that: during this period Duke Ellington and, later, Charlie Parker exposed the invalidity of assumptions that con- ventional harmony was clapped out.

Some years ago I went to see Roberto Gerhard, a musician whose work I revere, for advice on improvisation within a 12-note discipline. He made me play the clarinet for him, solo, which was a bit unnerving, but he was kind and, I think, interested. I'm still waiting for his bill. He told me to read Krenek's pamphlet on serial composition, but that I was certainly underestimating the problems of improvisation within the Schoenbergian limits: 'A lot more than conventional harmony has to be jettisoned to make it work.' I read Krenek's book and went back to Dixieland. As far as I could make out, if you had 12 musicians, they could have one note each to improvise with if you wanted to avoid breaking the rules about consonance. Pop music isn't worried about tee, its relations and progeny, largely concerning itself, not un- successfully, with other than abstruse harmonic problems.

Jazz *is* worried and in a bit of a state. You can hear some very different approaches to the matter on Radio-1 in the *Jazz Workshop* series on Wednesday evenings at 9.15. None of these, thank goodness, are predicated on 12-note dogma. Some of the musicians involved, notably Kenny Wheeler, base their assault on subtle refinements of conventional harmony and modal excursions performed with style and technical excellence. Others, like Mike Westbrook, seem to be playing the whole thing by ear, eclectically assembling components furnished in the recent past by Coltrane, Dolphy and Shepp. Hardly any of them fall into the tragic error of modern straight music, which eschews visceral appeal entirely. This confirms my suspicion that jazz is a superior all-round vehicle for aural entertainment, even for intellectuals. Looking confidently forward into the restructured Seventies, the BBC really should have done better than to relegate these programmes to late-night listening (after midnight on Sundays), which happens from the end of September on. Could have been worse: I understand the series narrowly escaped the chop. Whatever the opinions of the BBC or the British public on the status of the musicians taking part, some enviable international reputations have already been established. Last year John Surman, who plays baritone sax with Westbrook, won the award for the best soloist at the Montreux Jazz Festival. This year it was the turn of drummer Tony Oxley and Alan Skidmore, who led his own quartet on tenor sax.

7 May 1970

OLD-TIMERS

About eight years ago Eddie Rogers, then a song-plugger, was carpeted by his boss: the British rights to an American song had been bought for the company and Eddie's efforts to place it on radio and TV, while successful, had been unable to secure for it a respectable position in the UK charts. It was explained to Eddie, in the strong terms natural to desperate Tin Pan ailments, that the song had cost thousands, that it was now a hit in the States, but nowhere in Britain. What had he left undone simply to transfer a number one across the Atlantic? Seldom short of words, Eddie paused only momentarily before delivering one of the most stunning ripostes in history: 'Hitler was number one in Europe: he didn't mean a bloody light here.'

I saw Eddie shortly afterwards and an acetate disc was pressed into my hand. This was a rendering by Nat Gonella of a song called 'The Original Satchmo Blues', which turned out on the turntable to be a kind of despondent version of Louis Armstrong's 'West End Blues'. It seemed to me at the time that, in atonement, Eddie badly needed that joke if he was responsible—he wasn't likely to be responsible unless existentialism had suddenly burst in on him, which I doubt——for coaxing this great trumpeter to travesty both himself and his idol. Eddie phoned me to chase up the song and I suggested that Nat was a natural for *This is Your Life*, then on BBC. Sure enough, Gonella's story appeared about a month later. I was playing at Wood Green at the time and Nat joined in occasionally, phrasing his singing precisely like his trumpet-playing, relaxed and surprisingly dedicated. Drinking later, he told me about the TV show—his brother Bruts couldn't be bothered to turn up: 'he must be mad, he could have earned himself a score' (£20)—thus exhibiting a healthy cynicism about the show only topped by Danny Blanchflower, who dematerialised at the gate of immortality with no-expense-spared fly-ins from everywhere already practising never-to-be-remembered catchphrases in the wings.

Nat and the great trombone-player George Chisholm were the stars of the *Yesterday's Witness* BBC 2 of 4 May. This was called 'Whatever happened to music?' and couldn't easily have been surpassed either as an account of the times or a record of what the protagonists were and became. Everyone spoke their minds and even the late Jack Payne contrived to sound endearing while expounding his simplistic dictum that every eight bars must be made to count visually. A clip of film showed an acrobat cartwheeling in front of an intricate brass arrangement of 'Tiger Rag'. Profligacy was endemic in the Thirties. Chisholm told about Bert Ambrose contemptuously turning a ten-bob tip into sensible bunce by adding four pounds ten and refunding the then enormous sum along with the advice: 'Buy yourself a shirt, sonny.' Bert was soon to lose his, as did Harry Roy and many other heroes of the time by misjudging the speed and stamina of horses or the number of aces in a pack. In 1930 Roy Fox was head of production of Fox Films. Somehow he got an eight-week gig as a band-leader in London. He was seen by Jack Buchanan talking to the Prince of Wales (turning down a request for a tune, actually) and never looked back. Or far forward, for that matter: for years the Musicians Union have instructed me in their circulars that I mustn't accept engagements from Roy among others. I'd never seen him before the TV show this week. Not much jazz was featured in the show and the best of it, Louis Armstrong's 'Back o' Town Blues', was anachronistic, being a filed extract from the Sixties. But the jazz players—Gonella and Chisholm —and the one jazz writer, Spike Hughes, came out best. Chisholm is in any case playing as well as ever in spite of his comedy chores with the odious Black and White Minstrels (would blacked girls and white chaps be as offensive?), and Chisholm, playing well, is very good indeed. A fat, warm tone and complete though original technique identify him absolutely. One note would ensure it was no one else.

His sense of fun, obvious in his music, came through. When playing for Bert Ambrose all the brass had to wear mutes: background as opposed to the underground jazz Chisholm played through the small hours in clubs. But for broadcasts, due to primitive transduction techniques, the mutes had to come out, and as this was live, in hotels and such, apologies were made to the hooray patrons. With hindsight Chisholm invented a placard: 'Normal service will be resumed as soon as possible.' His graphic gifts are considerable. 'That,' said Chisholm presenting two clenched fists together to the camera, as if you had to pick which one the surprise was in, 'was *one* of Fats Waller's hands.' And you could see the great black hand caressing an octave and a half while the other reached out for John Haig.

2 July 1970

BLUE TURNING GREY

During World War Two the Workers Musical Association published a pamphlet called 'Background of the Blues' by the late Iain Laing. This gave a number of examples of archaic blues lyrics, together with some indication of the form that blues might be expected to take, and went on to bend the history of the medium unrecognisably to fit a theory, eminently acceptable to the WMA, that this was a music of the proletariat. Aside from music, however, the blacks' class background sticks to the meaning of the word. 'Having the blues' indicates a state of mind between simple depression and despair, but not everyone can have them without generating comic or offensive overtones. Things being what they are, the Archbishop of Canterbury and the Pope must be close to despair at times, but 'the Pope has the blues' isn't a serious statement.

Even in social extensions the blues, if not necessarily black, are exclusively American, and their literary expression is therefore bound to be less than fully comprehensible to those reared in other cultures. Quite apart from the false superstructures they build on blues lyrics, interested whites can shoot through sheaves of them without ever touching the sides because they haven't shared with blacks a complex and private childhood background. The ritualistic 'dirty dozens' game is particularly mystifying. This Epikastean accusatory discipline can be understood by the world's middle classes as a brutal, if didactic, children's frolic, but even after poring through hundreds of envenomed lyrics in the style of Speckled Red's 'Dozens', or reading Paul Oliver's lucid account of the ritual in his book *Screening the Blues*, whites can feel little but shock impact from the tirade of incestuous insults. Until the permissive society blew in there was no bridge joining black and white even over the troubled water of more ordinary sexual matters. While blues singers boasted continually about 'rolling all night' and compared their prowess to that of Stavin' Chain, the fabled black super-Lothario, or moaned about armies of seducers who'd been 'digging their potatoes', the sexual mores of bourgeois blues fans during the Thirties, Forties and Fifties excluded any possibility of real ideological contact.

As a teenager in Edinburgh I listened avidly with other young enthusiasts to recordings of the great blues artists: Leroy Carr, Kokomo Arnold, Roosevelt Sykes, Sonny Boy Williamson and a host of others. We understood some of the sexual imagery that formed the largest part of their blues repertoire, but could feel no involvement beyond a musical one in such an alien world. The best a successful Don Juan in our camp could hope for, far from being 'eagle rocked till his face turned cherry red', was to be granted a quick fumble round one of proud Miss Jean Brodie's charges on the Carlton Hill after dark. Whether the bigger misapprehension was that sexual appetites and gratifications aren't pretty evenly spread or that blues are mostly about sex because that's what blacks are mostly about, I don't know. It never occurred to us that sexual censorship was simply easier to buck than anything that was really bugging blacks.

In the Sixties pop's incursion into blues imposed a more stringent censorship, which it brought in from the mass media it depended on. Traces of voodoo, gambling, drugs and sex were permitted only if thoroughly disguised—and camouflage was becoming increasingly difficult. With hallucinogenic banana-skins and LSD about, you don't need much acumen to divine the 'hidden' meaning of 'Mellow Yellow' or 'Sugartown'. At the same time blacks could be more explicit about the consequences of their continuing oppression by whites. All this probably means the end of blues poetry as we know it: I wish it also meant a step in the direction of real emancipation. Having to work in an alien milieu imposes crippling restrictions. The Beatles' blues-type songs, for instance, have to use American imagery. 'I've got a ticket to ride': to where—Swadlincote? Or at least avoid native identity: 'Can't buy me love'. These lyrics don't compare with the definitively non-blues 'She's leaving home', although musically I find the songs better. They are hopelessly outclassed by *real* blues lyrics.

Musically the blues isn't just a form or a harmonic sequence or an agreed melodic series. It's a method, an approach, a *feel*. Previous definitions have usually started with form/harmony as follows: four bars tonic, two bars sub-dominant, two bars tonic, two bars dominant, two bars tonic equal a 12-bar blues. If this were the case, the riff tune 'In the Mood' would be the ideal archetype—which it isn't—because it uses only these chords in various inversions and in the correct sequence. The blues scale, so we're told, includes the flattened third, fifth and seventh. So it does. It also includes the major third, fifth, seventh and occasionally the flattened ninth. As these can be related to the tonic of any chord in a blues and as the flattened ninth, like the raised ninth (which is also the flattened third an octave up), may be incorporated for other than blues reasons, it's not unusual to use all 12 semitones in a blues solo. 'In the Mood', of course, doesn't have any of these blue notes: it's still a blues. The frantic virility of blues is now as amazing as ever. Ray Charles, who'd been an effete popular singer, came home to them, as did Berry Gordy, who started the best of all pop-blues productions (Tamla Motown) ten years ago. A cloud somewhat larger than a baseball glove looms, however, in the denial of their Americanism by some of the most gifted black musicians like Archie Shepp. This effectively means not playing blues, which have links with slavery. Considering what Americanism has denied Shepp and his race, it's reasonable. But I hope it's only a kind of strike.

19 July 1971

SAINT LOUIS

The BBC has been going through a really terrible time. For one thing, I resigned last week. Opinions will vary about the long-term effects of this on the Corporation but I should have thought it pretty shattering: a severe blow. Then Philip Jenkinson, in *Film Night*, whined about requests from jazz fans which he'd ignored. Wasn't his bag: not up on that scene, and anyway there wasn't much jazz in old movies. He followed this with a clip of the atrocious Raymond Scott band doing 12-finger exercises which amply established the non-credentials claimed. The Sunday movie, *Birth of the Blues*, drove his other point home: Bing Crosby re-inventing jazz for whites aided by an idiot bass-player who discovered pizzicato when his bow fell apart. The film's racism precludes a showing in countries other than those where *The Black and White Minstrel Show* has proved unable to start riots. But Louis Armstrong, the greatest soloist in jazz, delivered the final thrust by dying, two days after his 71st birthday, and some weeks after radio, exasperated by his recovery from a serious illness, put out an elaborately compiled obituary as a 'tribute'. Humphrey Lyttelton's past tenses must have puzzled and saddened any listener who, like me, switched on after the programme's start.

I didn't contribute to the obituary and won't write one now: I'm the wrong person to. As far as I can remember—and I can play or sing about a third of Louis's recorded output from memory—he could do no wrong: everything was perfect. Let me instead tell as accurately as I can my dealings with a man who was my god. What I hope this will contribute is some idea of the contempt in which white society held the greatest musician of the era.

In 1954 I wrote to Robert Ponsonby, then Director of the Edinburgh Festival. Would he be prepared to have Louis's All Stars as performers at the next Festival? He would, but he had to consult the Committee. Meanwhile I wrote to Joe Glaser, Louis's manager. He, in turn, wrote to Ernie Anderson, his European chap, copy to me: an illiterate letter, misspelled, telling us to 'keep it going'. Perhaps a Brazilian trip would fall through. Ponsonby faced opposition from Edinburgh puritans. Yes, he could have Louis Armstrong as a cabaret at the Festival Club—nothing more. Louis would have to entertain audiences, exhausted by culture, getting a few down them after hours in George Street. There ensued an extraordinary meeting between Ponsonby, Anderson and myself. Ponsonby, an ex-Etonian ('I remember Humphrey Lyttelton'), Anderson, representing Glaser (whose Capone-era ownership of the Sunset Café in Chicago had led to a lifelong friendship and a change of management for Louis), and I discussed terms. *Terms*: I was making 25 bob a week at the West End Café, and here we were, talking about £12,000 per week—half Louis's normal fee, Glaser asserted. Anderson added darkly: 'There's a whole lot of guys to be paid.' I couldn't cope and the deal fell through.

When Louis's All Stars arrived two years later at the Empress Hall —on a revolving stage, of course—I played with the band one night. I was introduced in the familiar gravel voice as 'that great trumpet man—Sandy Brown'. Understandably I fumbled nervously with the clarinet keys in 'The Saints'. 'Nobody told me about that—you playing clarinet,' Louis muttered. I didn't care: I'd played with him. On another occasion—Louis was being presented with something or other—I made a speech. So did other real fans like Nat Gonella. The main speech was made by the late Jack Payne, whose theme was that Louis must be okay, because he'd sold a lot of records and made a lot of money. Then Louis, who loved pomp rather than circumstance, gave a new trumpet to an Irish peer's wife. The lady had to be coaxed to play a note, and Louis carried on from there.

2 December 1971
WIPED OUT

Have you ever thought how well the uppercrust symphonic player steers clear of the geriatric wards? I mean, conductors in their nineties tottering around pointing sticks sound almost dangerous. But the old chaps keep going, audiences keep coming, and, quite honestly, many of the performances are beyond the range of younger artistes: so Pierre Boulez with reasonable luck has another half-century at the top. If he were a jazz player his chances would be decidedly less rosy, were he still alive to gamble. Consider the following major jazz musicians, chosen here for their proven ability to change the course of the music that followed them: Bix Beiderbecke, Jimmy Blanton, Lester Young, Charlie Parker, Clifford Brown. The arithmetic mean of their life-span is 32 years. Alarming. As Jelly Roll Morton put it, 'if the women don't get you the liquor must,' or (updating a bit) the automobile must—or another form of speed or its relatives among hard drugs.

Clearly any jazz player over 30 is on borrowed time, so 'Help a jazzman today' should be the cry. And how do their short lives affect attitudes to their work? Surely scarcity value alone must rise in a world where only a few moments lie to hand for creation? Yes, a Beiderbecke solo—eight bars will do—in a turgid Paul Whiteman record is like gold. Every magnetic tape within a hundred yards of Charlie Parker during his lifetime has now been issued to the public: all the retakes, all the mistakes—everything, as if a tiny cheep from Bird was a diamond. Well, wasn't it? Issuing absolutely complete Parker was no more than due reverence. Jazz is improvised, so that losing the essence of a great musician on record is, at best, careless. Every trace of fleeting creation should be a treasure held in trust.

I must now regretfully recount an act of vandalism unsurpassed in recent history. The BBC, having videotaped in Ronnie Scott's club a number of the world's greatest musicians improvising for a TV series, issued the series and then, after about 18 months, wiped the tapes. Some of the musicians involved (Miles Davis, Cecil Taylor) were in a crucial transitional stage at the time of the recordings: they never passed that way again. The altoist and jazz columnist Dave Gelly met with disbelief when he spread the news. Wiping these tapes was

genuinely unbelievable. What kind of person would destroy irreplace-
able art works? The department who made the decision also handles
(besides jazz and folk) Jimmy Tarbuck and that interminably
serialised joke about George Cole's boring dyslexia: jazz comes under
'Light entertainment'.

Ian Trethowan, Managing Director, Radio, turned up on the wireless to explain why 'progressive pop' was to be allowed stereo space
on Radio 3. Listeners had been demanding it. Unless Trethowan
meant just playing stereo records, listeners can demand away—BBC
Radio simply don't have the electronic mixing facilities or the time
to provide 'progressive pop' in stereo. Ian Trethowan gave me
the impression that he didn't know or perhaps didn't understand this.

So the Beeb stagger on in the belief that jazz is no different from,
although less popular than, the rest of the crud muzak on Radios 1
and 2 and that a new demand for hi-fi progressive pop—whatever that
means—can be satisfied somehow or other without a 16-track mixer
in sight. Listeners will wish them luck with their pop show: it can't do
much harm anyway. But in view of their irresponsible attitude to jazz
I suggest that all BBC tapes are in future sent for safe keeping to the
Jazz Centre Society. We simply can't trust comedians with them.

During the Second World War hundreds of historic recordings were
made under the heading 'V-Discs'. These cut across existing recording
contracts, Musicians Unions' bans and the like, so the grouping of
musicians was often excitingly different. Some of these discs are being
issued on German Decca (you can buy them here) under the heading
Die Grossen Stunden des Jazz ('V-Disc', presumably, still hasn't got
quite the right ring over there). So far the bands include the Esquire
All Stars (everyone you could name in 1943) and the Benny Goodman
sextet, which was at its very best round about that time. One volume
is given over to Billie Holiday and is essential listening.

13 April 1972

TIME AND CHANGES

A senior radio Wheel's wheels roll him in spasms, like tape reels on a
computer, through the traffic sludge east of Hanger Lane towards
Broadcasting House. It's a May morning in 1964, and *Morning Music*,
a precursor of Tony Blackburn and Terry Wogan, squeaks from the
car radio. Squeeze-boxes and xylophones wheeze and plonk through
Leroy Anderson and Toots Camarata melodies. Sid Phillips plays
castrated Dixieland, as he still does on the Muzak in your local.

Nobody records rubbish like this, so the occasional recordings allowed by the needle-time agreement sound out of place (better), causing flickering frowns on Wheel's face. Suddenly as the lights at Harley Street loom, there it is: a discordant note. As soon as the invaluable passenger is dropped at HQ bad vibes are spread and my band gets the sack yet again for playing too much jazz. No complaints. This happened about once a year and I'd been warned continually for playing too far out. But for the last three years, I've played too far *in* to get much of an outing on the only live jazz show on radio, along with a great number of jazz players in their late thirties upwards. When did you last hear Duncan Lamont or Dudley Moore on a jazz programme? Times change, and the avant-garde, who've been much favoured recently, are, it seems, to get a reduced quota in future.

I take no pleasure from the BBC decision. It's just another whimsical quirky switch. What's needed is a media policy for minorities like jazz fans: perhaps the Big Wheels can get down to this as soon as Parliament gets televised. We could then all see what the politicians' game was, and they could stop wasting media moguls' time by whining about the presentation of their personas, while a serious entertainment policy still hangs fire.

The main division in jazz at the moment is between those musicians who play time and changes (keep time and follow a set harmonic pattern) and those who do neither. The audience for the former, while a minority in mass terms, is quite large: that for 'free' jazz is small but enthusiastic. The time-and-changes group tend to be older and are tolerant of other methods. The avant-garde tend to be young and contemptuous of the time-and-changes lot. None of this matters except that the world will be a poorer place if the younger musicians aren't given a proper hearing, perhaps on Radio 3. I've complained before about putting jazz under the rule of the same chap who hires comics. When in December Robert Ponsonby succeeds Sir William Glock as head of Music, he should take the opportunity afforded by 'new broom' licence to inject some logic.

As for the negative behaviour of the ITV companies in this area, what can one say? Nothing, I'm afraid, that would bring the slightest improvement. Take Lew Grade. By his own account he gets into his office very early and stays late. That this differs from Maxwell Joseph's methods by about thirty hours a week may only serve to prove that ways of making money can't be codified, but if Lew spends more than half an hour a month on his programme-planning I know of two unemployed persons who could improve on that *and* ensure larger profits: Andy Capp and Flo.

At Ronnie Scott's there has been the Thad Jones–Mel Lewis band, an amalgam of time-and-changes and almost 'free' players. Time was never absent completely from Lewis, the co-leader/drummer, even during solo rubato passages, and changes were used by the brass but not quite by the saxes. The musical standards set were the very highest, but if I had to single one man out, it would be Quentin Jackson, the elderly, funky (almost pre-changes) trombone player, whose plunger mute growled at us like a wise, well-loved dog.

1 February 1973
NEW ORLEANS

Reeling towards the age of six after expulsion from the school percussion band for incompetence on the bells—the baby's rattle of kiddy instruments—I was brutally introduced to fantasy by my new professor, a Miss Patrick. Her claim to have attended every historical event, lava slopping about her in Pompeii, arrows plopping into her eyes at Hastings and so on, may have enlivened the lessons for other students, but they left the bell-ringer—wrongly guillotined, as Miss Patrick claimed to be during Thermidor 1794—with a scepticism I have subsequently found no reason to regret. Hence my distrust of the New Orleans mythology.

The story goes that here, in the delta of the Mississippi, a unique amalgam of racial traditions existed which led to the nativity of jazz music. Why something similar hasn't occurred in Bradford isn't clear. Still, the list of musicians who were born and raised in New Orleans is pretty formidable, including at least one genius, Louis Armstrong, and an almost inexplicable number of well-above-average players. Some of it can, I think, be put down to an insufferable arrogance endemic among Louisiana musicians. Corporate egotism gets music played as well as roads built and trains running on time—see under 'Third Reich'. The failing King Oliver, for instance, on being apprised of Duke Ellington's success in the early Thirties, remarked: 'Well, he's got Barney Bigard at his elbow telling him what to do.' Bigard came from New Orleans. It was unthinkable to Oliver that a genius could hail from Washington. And there are genuine traditions specific to New Orleans which had to be learned painfully by others. Slap-tonguing on reed instruments, a technique which produces pizzicato sounds without blowing through the horn, is one. Recently in New Orleans I heard a flawless demonstration of this by clarinettist Harold Cooper, a little fiftyish man with tiny legs, too small even for a diminutive body. I complimented him on the performance and said that few people are now capable of this trick. Again the arrogance. 'You're right,' he said without perceptibly employing face muscles, as he waddled off to get a drink. Perhaps Jelly Roll Morton was the archetypal New Orleans musician in this respect. His assertions, recorded faithfully for the Library of Congress when it became obvious that jazz was possibly to be taken more seriously than Meyerbeer, include gems like 'I invented jazz in 1903.' Morton's Red Hot Peppers are rightly regarded as one of the greatest of New Orleans bands. The trumpet player, George Mitchell, whose death in May 1972 went unrecorded in any journal at the time, was, however, born in Louisville, Kentucky, on the border of Indiana, and spent his life in and around Chicago. Mitchell was considered by the classic-jazz critical hard-core to be the superlative 'New Orleans' lead trumpet: Armstrong was suspect as being too clever and instrumentally adept.

Among the many other anomalies, anecdotes and myths, few are verifiable. I checked one. Buddy Bolden, the legendary originator of New Orleans cornet men, is supposed to have raised his golden horn to his lips on the shore of Lake Ponchartrain opposite New Orleans, swelled his golden lungs and blown golden tones into the still evening air. He was, this part of the Creole Nibelungen fable relates, 'callin' his chillun home'. I took the causeway across Ponchartrain and clocked 16 miles. As I stared in the driving-mirror towards the now invisible city, I decided to give Buddy every chance with climatic conditions, low humidity (difficult to concede in the Delta, but let's say there was a dry wind from the Rockies). Masking noise at the chillun's eardrums would be reduced—not much powered transport being about at the turn of the century. But allowing the benefit of all doubts, it was clear Buddy would have had to play about as loud as Grand Funk Railroad with their 7 kw of amplification to gain the notice of his chillun. Logistically, the legend made even less sense. Having received Buddy's message only 90 seconds after he'd delivered it, his chillun would need four or five hours at marathon speed rounding the lake on foot to catch the last few exhausted blasts of the master. No, it seems that Buddy as a superhuman foghorn, like John Henry beating the steam-drill by six feet, is a hopeful fiction. There remain the real achievements of the New Orleans musicians, who, by the end of the 19th century, were doing the kind of things, without thinking about it, that caught the attention of musicologists, about ninth hand, via the Beatles 60 years later. One last paradox: the Charlie Parker jazz movement stemmed from the work of Lester (Pres) Young. Nothing could be further, or so everyone supposed, from New Orleans jazz. But Lester ate chitlins and gumbo like the rest in his home town—New Orleans.

22 February 1973
TURK

'Earthquake McGoon's.'

'Is Turk there tonight?'

'The room is closed today, sir. It's the Indian holiday. Turk will be playing tomorrow.'

Hard to follow that. Trombonist Turk Murphy, of recent Irish extraction, leads a Dixie band in San Francisco's Chinatown. What Indian holiday? Not that Indians don't deserve one in this part of California: they must have eaten most of the dust in the Mojave Desert in the last half-century of Westerns. I put the phone down. I wasn't going to stay another day in Frisco and risk leaving my heart there along with liver, lungs and other vital organs in the event that the San Andreas fault cracks, as it must soon, and everything slips sideways. This time, unlike 1906, there would be no Spencer Tracy at hand, and the buildings have a lot more height to fall through. Also, compared with the 1936 movie, the quality of my requiem would be debatable. On the one hand, the movie had the first composition in his newly-adopted land by the man whose music came to enhance—or often to rescue—celluloid cowboy fictions in Monument Valley, Arizona: 'San Francisco' by Dmitri Tiomkin. (Remember his work in *High Noon* and *The High and the Mighty*?) On the other, there was the tradition represented by Turk Murphy. Murphy was a founder member of Lu Watters's Yerba Buena Jazz Band, formed in the early Forties.

Yerba Buena means 'good earth' and was the original Spanish name for the promontory on which the city stands and falls. The band catalysed the Dixie Revival. For the life of me, I don't know why. It played King Oliver tunes (with Bob Scobie on second trumpet, replacing little Louis Armstrong), but shifted the accent onto the first and third beats, which must have sounded very Teutonic to blacks, but persuaded thousands of young Teutons that this kind of music had a lot going for it. It was true that the musical qualities of the band exceeded those of most of their imitators: they played in tune and so on. But they had another, special, local quality, never imitated except by Graeme Bell's Aussies, which has more in common with the razmataz of Tiomkin's self-confessed imitation of Duke Ellington—which bore little relation to the master's work, as Tiomkin soon realised—than with the second- and fourth-beat accents from Africa governing the swing of the Oliver band. After Watters disbanded, the individual members took up a more ambiguous position with regard to beat accents. Scobie, who led one of the offshoot groups, died of cancer at too early an age. Murphy's band is the only remnant. He continues at McGoon's, Indian holidays apart, with an enormous scholastic New Orleans library of about four thousand songs, and hopes to visit the UK during a European trip in May. His clarinettist Bob Helm is one of the few who still squeezes an un-Goodmanesque noise out of the instrument, so I wanted to hear him. Instead, I heard Vince Catolicca, who lacks sight but not ear or technique, with Jimmy Diamond's band. Vince is one of the Goodman school, like Peanuts Hucko, Sol Yaged and about a thousand others. He, like most of them, has enough individuality within the imposed genre to lend interest to the clarinet. He had spoken to Benny recently, and Goodman, after some of the usual egocentric didacticisms, had to ask him to repeat his name. This didn't surprise Vince: nor would it any other Goodman-school clarinettist. It's like asking Zhukov to list his NCOs.

19 April 1973
LADY'S DAY

The legend of the boll weevil is an epic element in jazz history. For an animal that in full maturity just measures up to a grain of rice, it has a pretty fantoosh Latin label, *Anthonomus Grandis*. It lived up to it in 1921 by eating more than six million bales of cotton. What a nuisance. As far as jazz people were concerned, though, it was easy to identify with a creature who stole their livelihood in simply 'looking for a home', and the bo' weevil figures as an almost enviable aristocrat in blues lyrics because it found permanent residence in the unripe pod of the cotton plant: this, in a climate of share-cropping or short leases on property, respect and life itself, was, and is, an awesome feat. Miniscule researches haven't told me how much better the girl weevils fare than the boys—you can't call a 20-day-old adult a lady—but they lay all the eggs for sure, and more power to them for knowing how to do it where it hurts most, in the bolls.

Women have had a crucial role in African music, in the blues (as singers) and in the keyboard music of jazz. Not many took up wind instruments: but the ones that did include Melba Liston, Betty Smith, Kathy Stobart and Valaida. All of them deserve extended attention and I'd be particularly glad to hear from readers about Valaida, the black trumpetess who was active in the UK in the Thirties. More urgently, I cite Kathy Stobart as one of the great jazz sax-players. I do this because she can be heard in full bloom in the London area currently. The excitement in jazz music is usually concerned with nerve. You have to essay something that you are never certain to accomplish. Kate does this with minimum recourse to the store of assembled technical grocery to join up the uncertainties. Very few other jazz musicians can do without pre-learned punctuation. She's a Geordie, and as I last played with her on the night Sunderland beat Arsenal to Wembley, an analogue is appropriate. Arsenal's clogger, Peter Storey, was booked, which amputated over-the-top tackling from *his* arsenal for the rest of the game unless he was to leave his team with ten men by being sent off. Reduced to using skill, of which he is short although not devoid, he eventually helped to lose the game. Kate never uses anything but skill. In her present shining form, I recommend everyone, as a respite from wall-to-wall Mozart on Radios 3 and 4, to seek her out wherever she's playing.

Another lady, Lady Day (Billie Holiday), is topical at present. Berry Gordy, Tamla Motown's mogul, has produced a movie, now showing, which purports to be the story of Billie's rather brief life. The reviews have been universally good, mainly because of Diana Ross's performance in the leading role. Miss Ross was cross not to get an Oscar and, by all accounts, is justly aggrieved. Soon I hope to land the role of Irving Fazola, the great New Orleans clarinettist, in a Hollywood biography for which I'm writing the screenplay. I will put on 50 kg by crash eating and the story will be true, not the fantasy that Gordy's was. It will make Bergman look like Walt Disney and won't win an Oscar for anyone. What can jazz-lovers get out of the Billie Holiday film while they wait? Well, the Verve record label have already started issuing everything they have by Billie. The first album (of ten!) is *The Voice of Jazz*: Vol. I. The material was recorded by Norman Granz at his 'Jazz at the Philharmonic' concerts. All of Billie's work is superb, and when every other record company follows suit, as will certainly happen, no nuance of this great singer's recorded output will again be trapped in inaccessible archives. So Gordy's schmaltz has done us a favour, after all. Jazz players now know what to do to gain recognition: die, preferably under arrest—and soon.

It was a grave disappointment to British viewers (I'm told) that their entry for the Eurovision Song Contest only came third. Kind foreigners expressed the view that 'Power to All Our Friends', in spite of its meaningless lyric and paralysingly decrepit melody, was the 'strongest entry' since 'Puppet on a String' sung by dreary Sandie Shaw. It seems incomprehensible that a song which was sung by snow-white Cliff of Dover so many times on TV and radio couldn't make it. The Beeb took no chances either: on one occasion the song was sung, in recorded form, of course—or '†', as the *Radio Times* used to put it—and was immediately followed by a video recording of the same performance—that might have merited '††'. What went wrong? One explanation might be that even where talent is a serious disadvantage the performance should be entrusted to a girl. Through the ages women have had to learn how to make something out of nothing.

31 May 1973

DANSKING IN THE DARK

I came to my senses in a nearly horizontal position with my face six inches from a polished timber floor. Bang. No serious injuries, but a number of facial contusions which were embarrassingly difficult to explain: 'I walked into a floor.' I'd been sort of sleepwalking naked. When mopping up the blood it dawned on me where I was: in a largish house in the suburbs of Copenhagen at 5 a.m. Later that morning I resolved to have a relaxing day, as I faced yet another six hours of clarinet-playing in the evening. I read the morning paper, noting that *mælk*, *brod* and *flode prisen* had gone *op*. Snap. As I couldn't under-stand much else except .the tantalisingly repetitious 'Watergate' separated by metres of unpronounceable text, I moved to my host's library, selected some yellowing Danish journals on jazz music, and ambled into a garden. After being reminded of a number of unjustly neglected European jazz players of the Thirties and Forties (André Ekyan, Hubert Rostaing) and wondering what became of them, I pulled open a page to reveal a poor photo-reproduction of Valaida Snow, the black trumpet-playing lady. This was the woman I'd asked about in my last *Listener* piece, which tried to show that in jazz, as in other creative arts, women *do* count less. It was obvious that the anonymous reviewer—*circa* 1948?—thought that her reputation was going *op*, and that she had lived and worked in Copenhagen for a time, as Ben Webster and Dexter Gordon do today, but the details escaped me, so I underlined the bits I wanted my host to translate when he, in turn, got *op*, after an equally heavy night. But in the event Valaida slipped my mind: I was kicking myself on the plane to London of course.

When I arrived I found a highly literate account of Valaida Snow's performance and capabilities in a letter to me written by a *Listener* reader, Ken Stewart, who played drums in a band accompanying Valaida on one of her tours of Europe. In this case it included Holland, Switzerland and the UK. The band was formidable: Johnny Claes on trumpet, Derek Neville on saxes, and Reggie Dare on tenor sax in the front line. Ken explains that 'her playing had "authority"—as they say in the jazz books.' This rather endears Ken to me because jazz books, though plentiful, are usually full of meaningless words like 'authority'. But I quote further from his letter: 'Some of her solos were very well constructed and interesting, with a good attack and fine tone—when she was in the mood.' The last six words try to tell a story which most jazz musicians know very well. In any improvised medium, the success-failure ratio will be low, for reasons not suscept-ible to scientific study at this time. *Any* success should therefore be welcomed because it's pretty easy for a trained musician to play passable Bach/Mozart/Beethoven/Wagner/Schoenberg/Stockhausen. It's something else to stand in front of 3,000 or nearly nobody and compose it.

I'm afraid this brings me back to Denmark. I toured with a Dixie band (what else?) who had laboriously learned some of the numbers I had composed 20 years ago. I couldn't remember them and had to be reminded by listening to records (of mine) which I don't keep. It took me some time to persuade the band I toured with for ten days that jazz is an improvised music, and that I'd rather they played what they were going to anyway: I would fit in. *That* got through, but I still had to play 'Everybody loves Saturday night'—an African tune I stole from blacks—twice every night and, understandably, four times on Saturday. Denmark is banjo-land. No banjo: no good. The rationale —as expressed by an intense young Danish clarinettist—goes like this: mainstream music is a bastard quantity. It's a mixture of traditional and modern jazz. When I put it to him that his hypothesis meant that the late Johnny Hodges would, in 1935 or thereabouts, have had to invent what Charlie Parker did ten years later in order to play what he did, he retired hurt but not convinced. Woolly thinking still goes on in jazz and pop in the same way that Deryck Cooke, for the classicists, took up swords for the Beatles without having the faintest idea about their antecedents.

It must be time I left readers on an optimistic note for once, so here it is: Stan Tracey, who appeared in the recent jazz outpourings at the Almost Free Theatre, is a genius. Ian Carr, himself a fine musician, says so. *I* say so, and I will tell you why within a month. Furthermore, still on the *op*, Kathy Stobart, the gorgeous Geordie, told me Sunderland would win the Cup: I won too—I collected 25p from my son on her advice.

12 July 1973

A HARD TIME

If it isn't jazz, pop, folk, pibroch, raga and so on, what is it? You can't call everything in Western European music 'serious' because most of it wasn't. 'Classical' is even more inapt. 'Establishment' is a term which admirably suits current audiences for the genre, but is less than fair on the long-deceased composers or the quality of their often revolutionary musical concepts. Why one should differentiate at all is a question shrouded in sociological mystique. There's no doubt, though, that the powerful claque which has unloaded oceans of mainly 19th-century European music through the media has been reinforced by numerous performers already committed to other aspects of music. Such as jazz. Three prominent examples in the UK must suffice: Humphrey Lyttelton, who classified jazz ten years ago as a 'minor art form' (perhaps confusing the most virile form of contemporary music with his own second-division version of it), André Previn, a below-average jazz pianist who found it easy to switch to a higher rung in 'fleshpot' music—or whatever it's to be called; and Lord Trend of Wavendon (Johnny Dankworth) whose contributions to culture owe more to the musicians he employs than to his ability. The UK, in both Establishment and popular circles, has always been in the van of this Victorian–Germanic movement, even under the severest pressure: it would have been taxing the ingenuity even of Richard Nixon's press secretary to think of using Beethoven's Fifth as a victory anthem against the Germans. But that's too simplistic a grouse: the troops were singing 'Lilli Marlene' at the time.

Seeing the other point of view is alleged to be very British—sorry, English: I never experienced it in Scotland. Hans Eysenck has recently discovered how spurious this can be. Having found, in reasonably vigorous scientific tests, that Negroes and domiciled Irish scored lowly in IQ, he was set upon by undergraduate heavies. By all accounts he is recovering well but won't lecture for a while. Student leaders, who after all are supposed to be brainy, would do better to attack the IQ criterion for its exclusions, than elderly scholars simply relating what the tests measure. The truth is that IQ is dead. You can tell by feeling its pulse: it hasn't got one. IQ tests apply time as a quantity, but not rhythm. So the Negroes are involved in a game which ignores their major talent. Eysenck would have no quarrel with that if anyone had bothered to put it to him. Time—or rhythm, as it's called by those who don't fully understand it—is essential to the Negro psyche. This is one quantity that can easily be measured accurately in 0.001 second steps using a digital event-recorder. If you apply this to music, Count Basie's Band of the Thirties, Forties, Fifties and Sixties wins hands down over the Berlin Phil. It wouldn't be difficult to incorporate this aspect of time into IQ tests: Eysenck must have thought of it and, to this extent, he is guilty of telling something less than the available story. No doubt he will put it right on reading this. His detractors will continue to clap inaccurately on the on-beat beat and to thump people who are trying to find out things.

Rhythm (time) isn't as illegible as Fats Waller made out by answering when questioned: 'If you have to ask, you ain't got it.' It's the ability to know exactly, to one-fifth of a millisecond, where the pulse is in any time signature. As a soloist, one's contribution can stray from the pulse by a factor of up to 1,000, but the persistent and precise knowledge of when the pulse is due must be ever-present. Another exciting two years of research in store for Eysenck which should aid his recovery: glad to have been of help. A good example, as always, is Louis Armstrong. Listening to the 1925 recordings with Fletcher Henderson's Band you can hear young Louis after a flurry of fast execution by other soloists, placing just one or two notes where they happen to count most.

In the UK, almost everything one hears from Stan Tracey emphasises how well he has mastered time. As an introduction to the playing and composition of this genius I recommend his *Under Milk Wood Suite, Free on One, Perspectives* or *Latin American Caper*. I almost forgot to say that none of these albums (as any other examples of Stan's work) is currently available at your record store. Tracey's idol, in his youth, was Thelonious Monk, a pianist who could make a Steinway sound as if the strings were made of lead, who had a unique approach to harmony, and whose time (arpeggios apart) was impeccable. Building on this improbable foundation, Tracey is now producing music that is itself original and vital. His mastery is as elusive as that of Louis Armstrong and Duke Ellington: which is to say that it eludes those whose concept of time and pitch is less

accurate than the great players of jazz music and those who understand their work. Among the latter must now be counted Derek
Jewell of the *Sunday Times*, and the *Melody Maker* journalist who
considered George Melly's appearance at Ronnie Scott's to be a
wonderful blues session. George knows less about the blues but
probably more about showbiz than Vesta Tilley did. He will also get a
better obituary from the British press than Tubby Hayes, arguably
our best tenor sax player, did when he died recently at 38 having just
endured a second major operation for the replacement of a heart
valve. So Melly should consider this assessment as good news in the
general context of British jazz: he must count his blessings as must we
all who are not black. If only we could keep time too.

15 November 1973
SACRED CONCERT

24 October was United Nations Day. As Centurion tanks battered their
way towards Ismailia and Cairo in defiance of a UN Resolution, as
untold numbers of Peruvians, Ugandans and other expendable
humans of all hues were being murdered, Dr Abbott, the Dean of
Westminster, read out the Preamble to the UN Charter in the echoing
and uncertain acoustics of the Abbey. The deferential silence with
which the standing audience greeted this highly irrational document
qualified all those present to represent Sardonica at the UN. I had
spotted Ray the Pieman, the Egon Ronay of London's pie-stalls, as
soon as I entered. Like me, he had come to hear a Sacred Concert given
by Duke Ellington and the John Alldis Choir in aid of the UN Association. Ray's demeanour led me to believe that he had got outside an
awful lot of beer, so I didn't sit beside him, thereby avoiding much
profane chat when Duke's band weren't actually playing in what was
largely a choral work.

That he and I were in church at all was a unique event. We were
driven there by the fear that Ellington, at 74, might stop soon. When
he does, it will mark the end of the greatest musical career in the 20th
century. No opportunity, however unpromising, of glimpsing his
genius can safely be missed. The Sacred Concert, specially composed
for this event, was, however, distinctly unpromising. My ticket read
'Unreserved Nave £1.00 No View'. It would have been fair to add:
'rotten acoustics too; audibility further diminished by 30 clergymen
barging about, shuffling their feet, and mumbling'. The results, as

always with Ellington, were beautiful and rewarding. It's simply not possible to expect definition in this kind of acoustic climate, so any tempo above 30 bars a minute loses impact. Ellington rightly refused to allow this to deter him from using faster tempi, and often got round the difficulty by separating the brass stab figures by a long enough period to replenish silence before the attack. The sax passages were less successful, not through their complexity—though some were as intricate as Duke's late-Fifties sax scoring—but because the amplification was poor for the reeds: only Russell Procope and Harry Carney really came through. Procope's chances were aided by his use of the Albert system clarinet, which is a lot harder to finger than a Boehm (and therefore considered outdated), but at least has the holes in better places from the viewpoint of timbre.

In New York in August I was with Joe Temperley, one of the best baritone saxplayers in the world. Brought up in Cowdenbeath, he now plays with Deodata of 2001 and *Rhapsody in Blue* fame. Duke's band were playing at the Rainbow Room and I suggested a visit, fully knowing that the middle-aged business clientele would adversely affect Duke's programming: old favourites, medleys and so on. Joe said: 'Don't go. The band's not what it was.' I'm sorry to say that he's right. This great band *is* in decline by the superlative standards set by Duke himself. Paul Gonsalves is sick, Johnny Hodges dead, and the wonderfully diverse brass team mainly replaced. At the highest level, jazz musicians are just as scarce as any: not even Ellington's ingenuity can overcome the shortcoming, once his strength, that he writes specifically for his soloists and that the newcomers don't match the quality of those lost.

At Westminster, though, there was a bonus. Alice Babs, a Swedish grandmother, was a solo vocalist. This extraordinary woman has a perfect voice for Ellington's most plangent melodic lines. She has appeared at many previous Sacred Concerts by the Duke and he uses her talents more comprehensively each time. After his first and last visit to church, even the Pie-man was silenced by her performance.

～ 4 ～

Letters to the Press

FIGHTING FOR JAZZ

The Editor,   6 December 1962
Scene

GREEN AND COLEMAN

Dear Sir,

Benny Green is one of Britain's most articulate musicians. It is distressing, therefore, that his natural verbosity often conceals views of staggering naïveté, frequently classifiable under pedantry and/or irrelevance. Taking pedantry first, on the subject of John Coltrane and Ornette Coleman, how about this Butlerian gaffe? (*Scene*, November 24th) 'resolving one harmony into the next . . . is the best tyranny we have.'

The fight to retain the status quo is a common enough reaction among musicians trained in one school on finding someone has suddenly changed the syllabus; (and this, dear Ornette Coleman fans, is why the conclusions adduced by Green from the opinions of established musicians are almost valueless). You will recall, no doubt, with varying degrees of repugnance and nostalgia, the vaudeville classic about Beethoven and Wagner, who were said to be mad. In Benny Green's version, Mr. Bone's solicited punch-line would, I suppose, read: 'they were right—Ornette *is* mad!' He may be, but not for ditching Wagnerian harmony. Schoenberg did that fifty years ago.

More cogent objections to Coleman's method might have been that the ditching process is fragmentary, or that no obvious new discipline has emerged. I believe these too are specious, for reasons inexplicable within the confines of your letter columns. However, I commend to Benny's attention the following three statements of fact:

1. A handful of talented jazz musicians are dissatisfied with the restrictions imposed by Wagnerian harmony.

2. They are trying to do something about it.

3. Music will never be the same.

So much for pedantry. From the same article how about this for irrelevance: 'the chief defence of Coleman is that he is sincere. This implies . . . that I am not, and that Sincerity is all'? Of course it does nothing of the sort. These erroneous assumptions are then hurled, in the next paragraph, into a discourse on Genghis Khan! Own up, Benny!

How long must we wait for the inevitable agonising re-appraisal? Guessing, I give Benny three years to unload his traditional (yes, traditional!) prejudices. It's no skin off my nose. I can hardly follow the changes in 'Tin Roof Blues', as Benny Green well knows . . .! I like Duke Ellington, though!

Sandy Brown

MAX'S CLARINET LESSON

M. Jones Esq.,   30th June 1967
Melody Maker

Dear Mr. Jones,

I don't know what happened to the clarinet in the recent course of jazz, but rummage as you will through the hardware hanging on Roland Kirk you won't find one, and outside of dixieland bands they seem to be pretty thin on the ground generally at the moment, so the majority of virtuoso jazz on clarinet is now rather venerable.

The one performance I would pick out as the most outstanding of its type is Barney Bigard's thirty-four-year-old classic 'Clarinet Lament' with Duke Ellington. Duke originally wrote the piece for him as 'Barney's Concerto', which describes the form of the piece. Bigard's command of the instrument is complete and mature, and Ellington had recently achieved the orchestral mastery and invention that still seems inexhaustible. The combined effect in the performance is staggering.

You can always tell an Albert system clarinet from a Boehm by the tone. The Albert gives a much fuller sound, particularly in the lower register. This is a result of the instrument having fewer tone holes and having them better sited acoustically than in the Boehm version, the only problem being that you really need tentacles instead of fingers to play anything complex on the Albert clarinet.

Bigard's technique is therefore even more amazing than is apparent at first hearing. He persuades the full tone of the Albert through a

Sandy's Christmas card to U.S. acoustician and Sheriff of Laramie Dick
Bolt. 'Wanted' are other internationally known acoustic experts.

series of difficult runs at breakneck speed without ever giving an impression of strain.

By the way, you can compare the tone of the Albert and Boehm clarinets in much of Ellington's work in the last few years. Russell and Procope play Albert, and Jimmy Hamilton Boehm. It's also clear from this that out of the hands of an exceptional virtuoso like Bigard the Albert is a much less agile instrument.

Barney had a chequered, and not frequently satisfactory musical career before and after his Ellington period, so it's fortunate that there are ten years of recordings of his genius in that most appropriate setting. Woody Herman and Tony Coe owe a debt to Bigard but he influenced only a few later clarinettists probably because his best work was almost contemporaneous with the Goodman era. That was a pity. It seems to me that Barney at his best was unbeatable.

Yours sincerely,
Sandy Brown

B.B.C. Jazz

The Editor,   9th March 1973
The Listener

Dear Sir,

Radio Jazz

Mayne and Rush independently compared my playing (unfavourably) with that of the late, great Sidney Bechet (*Listener*, letters 8th March). They are entitled to their opinion which I take as a poetic compliment (the comparison with the incomparable Bechet alone, that is)—in a 'Jenny kissed me' vein.

Everything they said about the BBC's invisible policy on jazz is true, and Rush, in particular, pin-pointed their appalling irresponsibility in referring to the notorious case of the erased videotapes. I mentioned this a long time ago in a *Listener* piece. For those who can stomach brutality it bears repeating, and beggars any more description than the facts. The BBC, in gay mood for once, videotaped a series of programmes by great jazz musicians of the era. They transmitted the shows, and after time elapsed, some of the performers died through various misadventures not unconnected with their tribulations in pursuing this persecuted Art. The BBC then deliberately erased the tapes. The decision to wantonly destroy Art was made by a senior figure in the Corporation whose star still shines brightly there, but, I hope, nowhere else. All Rush's questions deserve a reply, but I can answer one: Robert Ponsonby, the new Controller of Music, is responsible for BBC jazz, as he is for *all* forms of music. Take heart, readers, from his fight fifteen years ago to get Louis Armstrong in the Edinburgh Festival. Now he has a harder fight. Encourage him. He lost the first one through lack of support.

Sandy Brown

The Editor,   22 March 1973
The Listener

Dear Sir,

Radio Jazz

Rod Hamer's letter (*Listener*, 22nd March) is hard to follow. He seems to be saying that jazz is (would be?) better off artistically if it weren't subsidised. Let's be clear about this: it isn't, unless he considers less than one twentieth of one percent of the Arts Council's annual dispensation a 'massive hand-out'. He suggests, however, that by compromising 'a bit' things will be okay.

Alex Welsh has a fine Dixie band containing excellent jazz musicians. At the same time Alex's vocal equipment is known to be atrocious. So if Alex singing 'Babyface' on Eric and Ernie's show is the 'bit' of compromise required, Rod's structures on aesthetics should be viewed with considerable suspicion. As to the bridge this compromise forms 'between artist and patron', I commend to his attention an analagous bridge between patron and servant illustrated in Wally Fawkes' current Flook series.

I must assume that Hamer doesn't like formal recognition of jazz musicians. What escapes him is that this is inseparable from attitudes to the status of the music itself. Jazz clubs (which he likes) have pianos which are uniformly out of tune and usually scrap. Another working compromise? Jazz musicians are denigrated, abused and underpaid. God for their soul? Howard Riley, an adventurous and capable jazz pianist, can attend a 'serious' (Hamer's word, not mine, thank goodness) music session on BBC Radio and be paid more than twice the fee offered for playing jazz. Keeping Riley's jazz abilities 'lean'? Jazz musicians don't like being forced to play out of tune, play rubbish, or be treated as idiots, but that isn't the crucial point.

The public are denied access to jazz music by the media. As Miles Kington pointed out (*Listener*, 15th March) no-one at the BBC had bothered to answer this charge because it's irrefutable. (I shall come to Howard Newby's long-awaited answer in a moment.) If Hamer really loves the music, he should support those who are trying to change this situation instead of indulging his muddled and contradictory philosophies in print. The last thing jazz musicians wish to do is to deprive straight musicians of the 'massive handouts' currently withheld from themselves. That, in Hamer's vernacular, would make straight music an exceedingly lean animal, as every symphony orchestra, opera and ballet company would vanish overnight. What they *would* like is that a glaringly obvious imbalance be rectified.

Sandy Brown

The Editor,   30 December 1974
The Listener

Dear Sir,

Rock on Radio 3

Fed on an exclusive literary diet of your publication, which many of your contributors also incessantly regurgitate in the Letters page, it would have become clear beyond doubt that the centre of a very flat earth is Vienna, and that the inverse square law applies both geographically and chronologically from the 19th century in that wasp's nest of thought. Since John Peel and I stopped writing in the *Listener*, such pieces as have appeared on Pop or Jazz have followed this ludicrous pattern. I hasten to add that lots of people write better on these subjects than John Peel or myself, and Tim Souster is one of them. Michael Chanan (12 December 1974) is not. But your readers will want some evidence adduced to support this hypothesis. Very well:

1. Lovable Derek Jewell's over-simplified over-simplifications are indeed ignored in public discussion on radio or the press. Although these shortcomings have been well known to jazz and rock artists for many a year, there isn't much musicians can do about it—which is why no explosives have been used nor guerrilla warfare embarked upon. Jazz and Rock lovers have just given up. Who could blame them? The programme *Sounds Interesting* certainly doesn't merit 800 words from Chanan: one would do, and it has already been used so often in this context that its currency as an expletive is endangered.

2. Rock grew out of black music from Africa. It has a long and distinguished past, which has been fairly adequately described

by Günther Schüller in his book *Early Jazz*, in terms that any Viennese would readily understand. Stockhausen, thankfully, had nothing whatsoever to do with it.

There may be rock music beyond the range explored by Johnny McLaughlin but I haven't heard any, and Chanan is unspecific about it. I've played with McLaughlin and object strongly to his genius being denigrated in this oblique way.

Unfortunately, such is the dearth of Jazz and good-quality Rock on all TV and BBC Radio One through Four that it's unlikely any of your readers will be any the wiser unless they pursue the matter themselves; they have had, and will get, no help at all from the columns of the *Listener*.

Yours sincerely,
Sandy Brown

Swan Song

Sir Michael Swann   January 24 1975
Chairman
BBC

Dear Sir Michael

BBC Coverage of Jazz Music

1. I've written before, over a period of years, about the abysmally small amount of time given to this art form. I found in doing so that there is nobody responsible in the Corporation for handling the output of this music—at least no one who has any knowledge or experience of it. That goes for the 'Jazz Committee', whose members are culled from light entertainment and pop music. This body meets so infrequently that policy decisions on jazz are made without its advice or even its knowledge.

2. Such replies as I received displayed an appalling ignorance about the subject: that was only to be expected. What I found much more disturbing was that the normal guide-lines of *any* management were ignored. For instance, Robert Ponsonby is Head of Music. He doesn't have any say about jazz. That's like having a Director General who isn't responsible for Scotland, Wales or Lancashire.

3. Now, it's intended to cut the jazz programmes still further, by approximately one third. This far exceeds the overall cuts in programmes proposed for economy reasons. Furthermore, the savings are

1. West End Café, Edinburgh, 1953. *Left to right*: Bob Craig, Dizzie Jackson, Al Fairweather, Sandy and Jackie McFarlane.

2. 'The King of Jazz and his Queen'. Hunter Square Registry Office Edinburgh, 25 September 1954. In the background, Edinburgh horticulturist Chris Bruce and Sandy's brother Jimmie. (Flo Brown)

4. Sandy with Red Allen. (Flo Brown)

3. Sandy with Louis and Lill, at Earls Court, May 1956. Louis introduced Sandy as 'that great trumpet man.' (Flo Brown)

5. Sandy and Flo (*right*) with the Dutch Swing College Band and Neva Raphaelo. (Flo Brown)

6. On the road. Sandy and Al, 1958. (Flo Brown)

7.   The Fairweather Brown All Stars, 1961. *Left to right:* Al Fairweather, Brian Lemon, Sandy, Benny Goodman, Brian Prudence, Tony Milliner. (Bruce Fleming)

8.   'Didn't it rain!' Publicity photo with Bob Wallis, 1962. (*Melody Maker*)

9. Al Fairweather and Sandy Brown's All Stars, 1962. The Incredible McJazz line-up, *left to right*: Al, Sandy, Brian Lemon, Brian Prudence, Terry Cox (in background), Tony Coe and Tony Milliner.

10. Doing a bit of business with David Binns in 1969. (Sandy Brown Associates)

11. Publicity photo for 'Hair at its Hairiest', at Doug Dobell's record shop, 1968. (*Pye Records*)

12. Leaving the London office with chauffeur-driven cocktail cabinet for a partners' meeting in Edinburgh, 1973. (Sandy Brown Associates)

13. 'The World's Greatest Royal High School Jazz Band'. Sandy and Al's last concert together at the Royal High School in 1974 with Stan Greig on piano. (Royal High School Music Society)

14.   Sandy at the 1972 Edinburgh Festival. (*Scotsman*)

scarcely worth considering in financial terms. Jazz programmes are among the cheapest to produce.

If cuts are to be made, surely either of two courses should be pursued: (a) the cuts should be directed at programmes which are expensive to produce, thereby getting the best value out of what's left, or (b) the cuts should be evenly spread through the whole programme output which would at least share the sacrifices on a democratic and fair basis.

4. I'm particularly concerned about the cuts in live jazz music which will now only allow about one hour per week instead of an already grossly inadequate ninety minutes. This is a terrible blow to talented artists already on the breadline. It's also a serious threat to a cultural tradition second only to that in the U.S.A. British jazz musicians are acknowledged to be the best in Europe. How long this can carry on depends on an immediate curtailment to policies very close to persecution. May I ask you and the Board to consider this matter urgently? Thank you.

Yours sincerely,
Sandy Brown

Broadcasting House **W.1.**   18th February 1975

Dear Mr. Brown,

Thank you for your letter of 24th January, which was earlier acknowledged by my secretary.

I am sorry that you should be so concerned about the effects of the cuts, which we have recently had to introduce, on our output of jazz programmes. In making these cuts, we have tried, so far as possible, to keep a balance between various interests. Jazz, I think, has fared as well as could be expected. A cut of an average of three-quarters of an hour a week out of a total reduction of 51 hours of broadcasting seems reasonable and still gives jazz a greater share of airtime than most other musical minorities.

We are in fact now broadcasting roughly the same amount of jazz as in 1972, when 'Jazz in Britain' was transmitted fortnightly, as it is now. It is fair to point out, moreover, that, with the ending of separate services late at night on Radio 1 and 2, the retention of 'Sounds of Jazz', at a duration of 90 minutes, has been at the expense of general music programmes in the period after 11.00 p.m. on Sundays, some of which were heard by much larger audiences.

Similarly, we have done our best to retain as much 'live' jazz as

111

possible. The reduction will average only about half an hour a week. We accept, therefore, that jazz remains an important area of musical creativity but, at the same time we have to recognise that contemporary jazz attracts a relatively small audience which cannot really be equated with the following for many music programmes of other kinds. Our research shows, for example, that opera commands an audience five times as large as that of modern jazz. Our output of jazz is planned and organised by an inter-departmental committee (the Jazz Committee) and this, I think, accords well with what we know about the audiences for jazz.

Our programme cuts, as you may know, have affected television as much as radio. We regret the necessity for them, but it is clear that even with the increase in the licence fee which was announced on 29th January, we shall not be able to restore the programmes we have lost, and indeed, we cannot rule out the possibility of further limited cuts.

Yours sincerely,
Michael Swann

Sir Michael Swann
Chairman
BBC   February 27 1975

Dear Sir Michael

Jazz Exposure on BBC

1. Thank you for your letter of February 18 1975.
2. Of course it's easy to prove or justify whatever one wants by inelegant use of statistics: I would have thought the Beeb somewhat above that kind of thing. I worked for the Architectural and Civil Engineering Department, in close collaboration with Research, Design and both Planning Departments for 16 years. Not one of us would have dared to send off the kind of reply you gave me. You simply must do better. If, as you seem to imply, 'linear' measurements only are to be applied, in no way can these be considered respectable 'statistics'. You say, for instance, that only 'half an hour a week' has been hacked off live jazz broadcasts. Had you converted that into a percentage—which I did in my letter to you—the picture would have been so dramatically different that I find it hard to accept that my complaint has been more than doctored and ignored. But let us examine the situation concerning Opera. Your own research tells you that 'opera commands an audience five times as large as modern jazz'. Great Balls of Fire! That means that John Surman & Co com-

mand an audience right now which totals 20% of that for Verdi, Wagner, Mozart, Donizetti, Berg, Bizet and whoever. I would have thought that a statistic worthy of celebration. What about contemporary Opera, which I would have thought directly comparable? What are the comparative figures—even in linear terms—for Richard Rodney Bennett's 'Victory'? Or for any other contemporary Opera for that matter, if you have broadcast one recently. You could have a jazz band for 5% of the cost of *any* opera.

3. The personnel of the Jazz Committee contains so few jazz experts that it no longer deserves credence, if it ever did in the past. How often does it meet? A committee is supposed to commit something. Does it?

4. You are not broadcasting 'roughly the same amount of jazz' as you did in 1972. Check it out. You are broadcasting very much less.

5. Your last paragraph expresses a blandness that your strongest admirers, jazz fans included, will be discouraged by. I wouldn't bother writing if I didn't think the BBC to be the best vehicle for quality music, and the best hope for the maintenance of standards in the future. If you give up that role you will rapidly find that your reliance must be, in future, on a tacit acceptance of pap and the audience support that is consequently produced. So, in that event, what do you claim to do better than Capital Radio? They already do more jazz than the BBC does. What worries me most is that in what looks like a stereotyped letter you evince no appreciation of how hurtful it is for someone like me to write this. I suggest that you re-read my initial letter dated 24 January 1975. That told it all. Get an expert to deal with jazz if Robert Ponsonby won't. People from Pop Music or Light Entertainment Departments just won't do. Oh . . . and can I have a reply to *this* letter please, rather than one to a number of faceless people whose complaints are obliquely referred to in your last 'compendium', if that's what it was.

Yours sincerely,
Sandy Brown

FESTIVAL FRINGE

The Editor,   11th June 1974
The Scotsman

Dear Sir,

Duke Ellington's recent death and Louis Armstrong's a few years earlier deprived the world of two astonishing musicians. Jazz music itself was further denuded of its establishment: a baleful word, used, here, balefully. It's not well known that Duke and Louis shared another unenviable distinction: both were half-heartedly approached to appear at the Edinburgh Festival. Neither, of course, appeared, as their proposed activities would have been of a 'fringe' nature.

The 'official' Festival concerns itself with Established Arts. There is an inherent and vital omission in adopting that course: Jazz music is live. Moreover, jazz musicians don't, on average, live more than 44 years. Duke and Louis were exceptional in reaching their seventies (just). Jazz musicians must normally therefore be caught young: so they *can't* be 'established' in the terms the Festival Committee would use.

Never one given to useless criticism, particularly of Festival Directors, among whom notably Peter Diamond and Robert Ponsonby have tried pretty hard to inject some realism, I propose a solution which, in my view, satisfies the Establishment criterion, namely that the Jazz Centre Society, a non-profit-making organisation supported by the Arts Council, be given a chance to organise jazz presentations featuring great young jazz musicians from all over the world—some of the best are in the U.K.—at the Usher Hall and other suitable venues at lunch-time concerts during the Festival as part of the official programme. No use specifying 'promising young jazz musicians'—Louis Armstrong was a master at 22 years, Bix Beiderbecke at 18; Mozart, a noted improviser, died at 36. The Festival needs expert help and the Jazz Centre Society can provide it.

Any International Festival must remain dynamic or gravitate towards a moribund entropy like Bayreuth. Edinburgh has produced some of the best jazz musicians in the world and has every reason to display its pride in them.

Sandy Brown

PEDANTRY

CONCORDE

The Editor,   1st October 1973
Noise Control and Vibration Reduction

Dear Sir,

Rupert Taylor's piece on Noise and Sleep momentarily resurrected my alpha rhythms above their usual low delta level when, in conclusion, he pointed out that fluctuating noise levels are more disturbing than steady ones. Depends how fluctuating. I well remember attending a demonstration of sonic boom put on by a previous Air Minister, Roy Jenkins, at which no effort short of barbiturates was spared to induce deep slumber among the guests. They were plied with refreshments and food until chins became glued to chests and little could be heard over the foreground communal snoring level. At that moment it seemed propitious to compare real and artificial sonic boom for the benefit of the paralysed journalists and the future of the disastrous Concorde (now on rental offer as an alternative to Hertz and Avis).

The effect was interesting. The arrival and departure of sub-sonic aircraft (Comet IV's) was accompanied by opening of admittedly unfocused eyes and raising of heads. That of supersonic lightnings and explosions merely by shrugs of hunched shoulders and uninterrupted volleys of Z's. No EEG's were taken.

The lessons are clear:

1. Get your investment money into the Distillers Co., Vintners and Breweries.
2. Get hopelessly pissed before you go to bed. You will be hung over in the morning, of course, but the unsellable Concorde won't have woken you up as it flew about looking for customers.

Your faithfully,
Sandy Brown

CHRISTIAN ARCHITECTS

The Editor,   23 October 1973
Architects Journal

Dear Sir,

Christian Architects

I suppose they abound, although I haven't met any. But the Race Relations Board won't help regarding the advert to which Rosalind Sanders takes exception ('Secretary to Partner required in Christian Architect's Office') in her letter in the October 1973 Journal. I'll tell you why:

A friend of mine called Ken, who has had to leave the country for reasons of financial health, used to run a bucket shop operation on Sundays. This contravened the Sunday Observance Laws. He was prosecuted. 'Jews do it.' 'You aren't Jewish.' 'I'll *become* Jewish.' He then discovered that defining a Jew was somewhat difficult. It appeared, from enquiries at the Israeli Embassy, that you need a Jewish Mum: oy oy OY, Ken should be so lucky. Unfortunately he wasn't. But, thought Ken slyly, that must mean that Jewishness (or a waiver from Sunday Observance Laws in his case) was genetic, racial. So he put it to the Race Relations Board. Nothing. He was put in jail in Ealing and fined £900.

The Race Relations Act was designed to reduce exploitation of Blacks and, while not altogether successful, has helped a bit. It won't assist Rosalind Sanders. Nor would it have helped K. C. White and Partners who were responsible for the advert: they might have weaned away my excellent Jewish secretary if the money was good. But she didn't fancy the job. I'm not sure of her motives, but they probably contravene some kind of legislation somewhere.

Yours faithfully,
Sandy Brown

NIXON

The Editor,   12th September 1974
The Scotsman

Logic used to be a strong suit in S.E. Scotland. I suspect that it still is. That it's never mirrored in *Scotsman* editorials is something many of your readers just accept abjectly. I usually do, but your piece on Ford's astounding pardon for ex-President Nixon has goaded me. Consider the following scenario:

1. Unscrupulous Liar gains power by illegal manipulation of funds provided by known criminals.
2. Liar consigns 50 minions to jail, under legal processes, for misdemeanours committed by himself. Another 50 await trial for crimes which Liar demonstrably knew about and probably instigated. Liar denies culpability. Minions remain in jail.
3. Liar (by now in charge of the most powerful nation in the world) decides to buy the World clandestinely by entering into financially unfavourable deals with opposing countries, sells wheat at huge loss, etc.

116

4. Liar defies judicial processes and lies (what else?) about past.
5. Liar (also found to be 'incompetent') forgets to destroy tape recording concerning crucial proof of mendacity, having already re-edited other tape recordings so ineptly himself (no-one else to trust) that nobody is fooled.
6. Liar, on being assured of conviction and imprisonment *unless*, resigns from running the World badly.
7. Liar is totally reprieved and offered vast sums of money for an edited version of his lies.

If I took this scenario to Joseph Losey, a life-long opponent of Nixon, two weeks ago, he would have turned it down as incredible, and too meretricious to film. But it *happened*. He might think again now that the *Scotsman* has approved all the decisions involved.

What concerns me is that your readers may thus be encouraged to underestimate the American People. They should not. A large number of them, of military age, refused to accept the lies told by Presidents Johnson and Nixon about the objectives of the Vietnam War. They became draft-dodgers, and thereafter outlaws. Now that the lies are exposed they remain outlaws, but have the support of a large section of the American Public. Isn't that where our sympathies should lie?

Americans, with whom I've spent a concentrated month recently, are concerned about the Constitution. On this occasion (they recognise) it worked: were it not for Liar's incompetence in not destroying tape recordings, it might not have. Liar would still own the World: better Harry Secombe.

You will by now be aware of the role of the C.I.A. in Chile, Cuba, Vietnam and elsewhere (including the UK). This is part of the Executive Branch, and has been run by a Criminal President for two years—to put it mildly. Its budget would buy Scotland. *Do* something! Don't you have reporters or agencies? They are about to concern themselves with Scottish Oil. I'll leave it at that for the moment.

Yours faithfully,
Sandy Brown

~ 5 ~

Punting an Album

Despite his prolific output on record, the royalties from sales, as Sandy put it, hardly paid for the band's beer money. Even at the height of the Trad boom, he refused to play what promoters told him would sell records, and studiously avoided the formula often heard on the lips of the proprietor of the 100 Oxford Street jazz club as he tickled the ivories of the cash register, 'show me a banjo and I'll show you a profit'.

Sandy resorted to his own methods of drumming up a few sales. The record is *Sandy Brown with the Brian Lemon Trio*, recorded in 1971 at Trident Studios in Soho. Sandy designed the studios too.

Miles Kington Esq.,   5 November 1973
Punch

Dear Miles,

Herewith an album. I don't do many, so if you think it reasonable a line or two would help to break my sales record (8), thereby encouraging Doug Dobell. If not reasonable it's your turn to buy lunch.

Regards,

Yours sincerely,
Sandy Brown

Benny Green Esq.,   5 November 1973
The Observer

Dear Ben,

I enclose an album; some years ago I remember you saying that my playing was so inimical to the way you had been taught to play that you were unable to say much about it. Probably still true: still, you'll enjoy Brian Lemon.

>   Your Pal,
>   Sandy Brown

Steve Allen Esq.,   5th November 1973
London, N.1.

Dear Steve,
   At last. Another masterpiece. This should be filling the air waves at night. I leave it all to you: make me a millionaire.

>   Your Pal,
>   Sandy Brown

Alun Morgan, Esq.,   6th November 1973
Chatham, Kent

Dear Alun,
   This album is free. If you want a pint as well, write a few words on it for something or other. Adverse criticism will reduce the offer to ½ pint.
   See you soon.

>   Sandy.

The same approach was often used to drum up work:

Attn: Iain Mackintosh   11 March 1975
Theatre Projects Ltd
London WC2

Dear Iain,

Minor Projects

   Last time we met you asked me about collaboration on minor

119

projects on a time basis. We do this pretty often. I enclose a brochure and scales of fees. It's not infrequent for us to spend only a day or two on a minor project thus—we hope—forestalling a major disaster. It does one other quite important thing: it gets the designer off the hook on grounds of Acoustics, a subject which is usually raised to account for draughts down the neck, blocked drains and/or visible dandruff on the shoulders of the auditor sitting in front of you. I expect you think the last item to be a fabricated essay at a jokey reaction: I assure you that it was put to me by Mrs Yehudi Menuhin while her husband solemnly nodded his head.

So just get in touch when you need an hour or so. Hope that's of use to you.

Yours sincerely,
Sandy Brown

Miles Kington, Esq.,   3rd December, 1973
Punch
London EC4

Dear Miles,

Ian Carr & Graham Collier Books

900–1000 words coming up long before Xmas, full of jokes and yuletide cheer (as you would expect in a fun mag.) The fee of £40 is handsome, as I shall remind Karl. He may be submitting speculative copy to you after 1st January 1974 when his resignation takes effect at the Beeb: just couldn't stand all those crumpled suit alcies any more I suppose. Should Alcy be spelled with a 'k' like seltzer?

I'm sorry Charles couldn't do the reviews but rejoice that £40 can no longer tempt him.

I expect I'll get the sack from the *Listener* when Karl goes but I've been sort of hoping for that for years. See you soon: it's my turn for lunch. I enjoyed the Punch one but, as you say, it was rather angled towards the star guest,* and I found it a bit of a strain keeping up a flow of inspired wit all the time: I'd prefer to give someone else a chance to speak another time. I notice that rather taciturn geezer at the end of the table in the corner had every reason to be a bit gloomy: I had no idea he was a failed financier. It's nice

* Jeremy Thorpe.

to think that *Punch* feeds these hapless chaps now and then. A crust or two in one's belly must make it a mite easier to face sitting in a pathetic little City office waiting, please God, for the phone not to ring.

Yours sincerely,
Sandy Brown

- 6 -

Gentleman Jim

Not long after Sandy left Edinburgh in 1956 and came to live in London, an admirer of his, Jim Godbolt, became agent for his newly formed band, The Sandy Brown—Al Fairweather All-Stars.

Despite this professional association both relished sharpening their wits on each other, Sandy repeatedly poking fun at 'Jimbols's' cynicism and idiosyncracies and Jim was a master of the caustic rejoinder. This verbal duelling, often conducted with some asperity, but never in malice, was continued into their correspondence, much of which is lost. Sandy insisted that a succession of secretaries at the B.B.C. automatically filed anything vital in the waste paper basket.

Jim also ran a jazz club at the Six Bells, Kings Road, Chelsea. It was a venue for the 'mainstream' style, mainstream lying chronologically and stylistically between the traditional and modern schools. At 'The Bells' representatives of both schools happily played together, an experience that would be barred to them at clubs that were overtly 'traditional' or 'modern'. Between 1956 and 1962, roughly, mainstream jazz gained a considerable following, although never anywhere as great as for trad generally, and its commercial apex was represented by the 'Three B's': Acker Bilk, Kenny Ball and Chris Barber. At first Jim ran sessions four nights a week, but with the rock-and-roll revolution in the early sixties, jazz club audiences declined, most mainstream bands broke up, and he reduced the sessions to Friday and Saturday nights.

The Fairweather–Brown All-Stars had disbanded, Al Fairweather joining Acker Bilk, and Sandy suggested he put a pick-up band in on Fridays. Jim wrote to Sandy, confused the dates and complained:—'Furthermore, the financial structure you suggest entirely favours you and as you are forcing the issue I fail to see why the terms should be so overwhelmingly to your advantage, especially as the state of the business doesn't warrant financial speculation.' Sandy replied:—

Dear Jim,

Thank you for your extraordinary letter dated 21st June.

Firstly, let me put you right about holidays. I leave for New York on the 2nd September, not August as you had supposed. Perhaps you will check that I am not contracted for the first three weeks in September, and conversely that jobs are not being turned down for August, although it may be a bit late for that!

July 29th would therefore seem a good date to start, as I will have a clear month in the club before going on holiday.

Your complaints about the proposed financial structures lead me to wonder whether you have understood these any better than my holiday arrangements.

I proposed that the revenue should be spent in the following order:
1. Club expenses (approx. 8 quid)
2. Musicians' fees (16 quid)
3. Profit (whatever it is) 50% to you and 50% to the musicians.

Clearly the worst that can happen (if none comes at all) is that you will lose £8.00. The musicians will have spent at least that on booze. The break even point for you is 40 members (or 32 non-members). For the musicians this would be about 120 customers. This seems fair to me. You mention no counter-proposals so can I take it that you're just having a go or what?

The only action which would convince me that my suggestion is a bad or unnecessary one would be for me to have a residency on Saturdays. I already know your views on this. On the other hand I would be quite prepared to foot the bill for expenses myself, and fund the Friday night myself on an arrangement with the brewers; it was because of our friendship that I approached you about it. It was ethical to do so, but I was disappointed that it triggered off the abuse-apology-incomprehensible letter cycle.

If you have any counter proposals please let me have them.

Regards
Sandy

Dear Sandy,

Thank you for your reply to my letter of June 22nd which clearly you found 'extraordinary' on account of you not agreeing with its sentiments.

Alas, you have not been contracted to appear for any engagements for the first three weeks of September and had you been contracts for same would have been sent to you. There have been no enquiries for the band in August. I most fervently wish I could capitalize on your unique abilities, but these do not seem to have impinged on the public consciousness as much as you appear to think they do—or should—and I remain the poorer thereby.

I note that July 29th will be a suitable date for you to commence Friday nights at the Bells and despite current bad business I will go along with this providing we can agree terms. I must advise, however, that I am most reluctant to lose eight pounds, however trivial this sum may be to you, and that the band will spend this amount on booze is of no benefit to myself, nor my concern, except inasmuch that the length of time in excess of the agreed interval apparently necessary for the consumption of this eight quids worth frequently causes me pain and alarm, particularly in the case of its leader, one Sandy Brown.

Regarding the correctness of your action in discussing the matter with the Manager of the pub and two of my staff I must advise that I have a firm agreement with the Westminster Wine Company that no other entertainment takes place in that upstairs room without my being consulted; this because it is I who have built up the business to date, provided the bandstand, amplification and decor, part of which is a portrait of yourself by our mutual friend Bill Philby.*

This arrangement has been made with Mr. James, the company's Catering Manager.

I reserve the right to book the programme of my choice on Saturday nights and would not consider experimenting with this in order to prove my point about Fridays even if, in respect of the latter, I hope to be proved wrong—may it be that the mob will surge towards the pay desk once they know you are to be on the band-stand—between drinking, chatting sessions, that is.

As for my 'abuse' I wouldn't regard my relatively mild comments on the telephone as abusive, and I did apologise for raising my voice when some particular aspect of your considerable ego became more than my saint-like patience could stand!

Yours.

Jim

Openings for Sandy's music were very few, but he did manage

* This was stolen. Someone, somewhere, has a full-size portrait measuring approximately six feet by three of Sandy Brown.

to obtain a booking at Roger Horton's 100 Club on Oxford Street. The band failed to turn up and Horton, for the first time in the club's history put up the shutters. A wag scrawled across a 100 Club Poster bearing Sandy's name—'We Never Closed' mimicking the famous slogan of the Windmill Theatre throughout the war. Horton was not amused, but he did agree to give Sandy another booking that triggered off another round of testy correspondence. Jim received a copy of a letter to Sandy's pianist and fixer Brian Lemon.

Mr. B. Lemon
London N.W.6.

Dear Brian,

We have a gig at 100 Oxford Street on Thursday September 4th. Can you book chaps at suitable rates? Your telephone wasn't working to-day and Jim Godbolt seems reluctant to do more than pass on messages from Roger Horton and I thought a letter would be best but I am going on a bit . . .

Your pal

Sandy

Copy to Jim Godbolt Agency,
72/73 Dean Street,
London W.1.
(Don Kingswood).

Jim appears at this juncture to get his manager to ring Brian Lemon and fix the details.

Dear Sandy,

Have received, quite gratuitously, a copy of your letter to Brian Lemon, dated August 6th.

Your delusions of grandeur are something else! I am referring to your lordly suggestion that I 'get my man' to ring Brian Lemon regarding the gig at 100 Oxford Street. However, there is one sentence in that letter with which I am in complete agreement, to quote: 'But I am going on a bit . . .' Oh, indeed! In your case it was ever thus!

I would draw your attention to the correct spelling of Don's name. It is KINGSWELL, not 'Kingswood', as mysteriously bracketed under an incorrect address. It is several years since my office was at Dean Street and never was it at the non-existent address of 72/73 Dean Street. For someone with an eagle eye constantly open for the failings of others it would have escaped your attention that the numbering system on Dean Street is the conventional odds one side, evens the other, and the comings and goings of lesser mortals from whatever address would naturally pass unnoticed by your grand self.

Your good friend
Jim.

Jim,

It's surely not surprising I should send you a copy of the letter to Brian to confirm in view of an error of omission on your part in the recent past.

I've commended the attention of my secretary to your correct office (and home) address. Please convey my apologies to Don (his name will be spelt correctly in future) or do I have to write to him under separate cover?

I was amused that your secretary (as evidenced by the erased quotation marks and the substitution of lower case for the capital 'D') was under the misapprehension that I was somehow involved in an operetta called 'Delusions of Grandeur'. I'm sure she is now aware that this was no more than another of your regrettably frequent perjorations about alleged arrogance on the part of the world at large. Graham Burbige and Laurie Ridley went to Phil Robertson's funeral. I couldn't face it, although I'm one of the few people he didn't turn over. Most of the friends he dispossessed forgave him and he could certainly be forgiven a lot for claiming Higgins as his star victim. We shall miss him.

I don't know why I'm sending a copy of this to Brian Lemon, but we appear to have established some kind of pattern.

Your pal,
Sandy.

c.c. Brian Lemon.

S. Brown, Esq.,   10th September 1969
London NW6.

Brown,

I note that the mode of address in your letter of August 22nd is lacking the customary endearment. True, this endearment is generally hypocritical, but none the less welcome, even from an adversary. Can I now expect your reply to commence—'Sir'?

If there was an error of omission on my part (in respect of your non-appearance at Oxford Street on August 7th), yours was an error of neglect in that you knew an engagement was pending at that venue and that you personally discussed the matter of the personnel with Roger Horton on more than one occasion. In the circumstances I would have thought it encumbent upon you to make further enquiries from me, even, as to the whereabouts of a contract or notification of the date.

Maybe a case of Mohammed and the mountain?

Presumably you originally advised your MD (come in, Brian) of the date and he didn't raise any query either.

The fault, I think, is more yours than mine. You were advised of the date and you discussed it with Roger Horton.

Granted, my secretary could have construed that you are somehow connected with an operetta called 'Delusions of Grandeur'. The title would suite yourself admirably.

The paranoia you have previously alleged in me is aroused by mention of Phil Robertson's funeral. What am I to infer by such a mention right out of context?

Thank you for your prompt reply. Would that you showed similar alacrity in returning to the bandstand at the end of your intervals . . . but that is another matter . . . and indeed, who are lesser mortals to remind you of your obligations in this respect.

> Your pen pal,
> Jim Godbolt

c.c. Brian Lemon.

Sandy's reply extracted maximum advantage from a typing error in the letter.

Jim Godbolt, Esq.,   26th September 1969
London W.1.

Jim Dear—(which should generate even more casting about in search of secret and sinister motives but I find the vaudeville straight lines you keep feed me irrestible).

The 'We Never Close' episode at Oxford Street is now developing into such a daunting reservoir of tedium, particularly for our unwilling confidant Brian Lemon, that the admeasure of even slightly more chat will probably breach the dam and wash away much of civilisation as we know it. My regard for your agonising sensibilities compells me however, to relieve you of direct responsibility for the holocaust by forestalling the inevitable verbiage in your next composition.

Your ingenious invention of the word 'encumbent' from the verb 'encumber' (to get in the way of: embarrass; to be a burden to etc.) was uncannily opposite to the situation I would have found myself in had I requested details of the performance for which I was not quite contracted. It took me some time to grasp the germ of this brilliant pun: I mistakenly read the word as 'Incumbent' at first.

I was reminded of the hazards attached to seeking 'information' from you by the tragic history of a certain Ruby James* in the Mail (copy enclosed); the sub-heading 'Disaster' and 'Awful' struck home. I had wondered, too, why Jack Baverstock was sacked and was grateful to have this cleared up. It was distressing to learn that you and Don had to share thirty bob—I enclose my cheque for fifty in respect of the last engagement at Oxford Street.

I mentioned Phil's death in my letter because he had just died and was, at least at one time, a mutual friend. In order to avoid overheating the simmering paranoia you refer to, I will remember in future, to keep desperate subjects apart under separate cover.

I take note of your criticism of timing of intervals on engagements and will continue to give this close attention.

Your old pal!
Sandy.

10th December 1969

Dear Sandy,

Regret my hastiness in replying to yours of September 26th, if only to enquire the meaning of—to quote . . . 'you keep feed me irrestible'. You will grant that there is a grammatical fracture or so in the construction of that sentence. The word 'irrestible' is new to me and the Oxford Dictionary is also unable to help.

I suggest you write them one of your pedantic letters, pointing to

---

* Jim rather unsuccessfully represented a singer called Ruby James, although he did obtained a full page feature about her in the *Daily Mail* and a recording contract for the Fontana label for which Jack Baverstock was the A and R man, although his departure from that company had no connection with Ruby.

the omission and demanding that they rectify. To round off the jokiness of your letter, you omitted to sign the cheque attached.

Will you please rectify.

Yours sincerely,
Jim Godbolt.

c.c. Brian Lemon

12th December 1969

Dear Jim,

Thank you for your letter of the 10th December. I hope the enclosed cheque is now in order.

I was rather proud of the word 'Irrestible'. It means, of course (as the prefix, content, and suffix imply), 'not able to be set at rest'—which regrettably can also be applied to this interminable correspondence.

The Oxford Dictionary is a bit slow, as you know. I think it somewhat unwise to omit, from the circulation list, our chronicler B. Lemon, so I've rectified that too: I understand he has a publisher interested.

Your pal
Sandy.

The dialogue continued over many a drink and telephone call, but Sandy had the last word. After his death Sandy's widow, Flo, handed Jim a pottery mug with his name on it, and the message that Sandy had found it on a shelf marked 'rejects'. Jim has one final regret that Sandy did not live to read his own book (*All this and Ten Percent*—Robert Hale) recounting his experiences as an agent and jazz promoter. Jim explained that Sandy's response would have been that should he embark upon such an exercise again with his obvious limitations and lack of education, he would be glad to be of assistance.

⁓ 7 ⁓

Football Fanaticism

Scots have played major roles in almost every great English jazz band and football team since the war. Sandy was an active participant in several London Sunday afternoon sides culled from the Fleet Street and Soho drinking fraternity. His skills were at their best in the bar before and after the match. He claimed to have prematurely hung up his boots as an inside right, when the captain, knowing he had no right foot kick, put him on the left wing for three consecutive matches. His heroes were Rodney Marsh and Queens Park Rangers. Those who dared to extoll the virtues of other clubs were often seen to falter under the haranguing monologue or letter that followed:

David Allford,   18th May 1973
Yorke Rosenberg Mardall,
London E.C.4.

Dear David,

'Courage Where Your Feet are Pointing' Dept.

It goes not unnoticed that your hurried absence from the country ('Dictated but signed in his absence') coincides with the influx of friendly strangers from the North who have come to witness the trouncing of Alf Ramsey's cloggers by superior skill and endeavour.
2. Please note that the postmark on this letter is the 18th May—the day before the English Apocalypse. I shall be happy to accept 5 sheets. Should the unthinkable happen, however, I will reluctantly pay *you* 5 sheets. Draw: no bet.
3. See me Jimmie? Aw wir no awa' tae bide awa'. Right? Aw the gither noo: start on doh—or doh flat—yin twa three . . .
4. Goals being of little significance, I predict the final score as follows

130

Football Fanaticism

		Storey	Bremner
(a)	Over the top tackles	29	3
(b)	Running opponents off the ball	68	4
(c)	Retaliation	1	278
(d)	Punching	432	790
(e)	Knee in the groin	1,761	1,761
(f)	Handling the ball on ref's blind side	4,575	8,243
	TOTAL	17,000,001	17,000,002

—a clear win for Billy Bremner and these fine lads from the glens and straths o' Bonnie . . . (cont. p. 894).

Your Pal

Sandy Brown

Yorke Rosenberg Mardall,   3rd September 1972
London, E.C.4.

For the attention of: Mr. D. Allford

Allford,

Having foiled, by expert control of my high-powered motor cycle, your attempt to crush me into the tarmac of the Britannia round-about, I've decided to take you and Ike Horovitch to lunch. A refusal will generate a police action for driving to the danger of the public and an anonymous bomb scare at Hillsborough prior to Sheffield Wednesday's most important game of the season (v. Q.P.R.). My secretary will fix this up—and lunch.

The theme of our luncheon discussion, culled from the writings of E. Powell, will be 'What are these Black Buggers going to do with Africa?' No doubt you will have some notes ready for our discourse.

Yours faithfully,

Sandy Brown

Mr. Ted Glendinning,   2nd May, 1974
Edinburgh

Dear Ted,

Rowdyism at Easter Road

Firstly I want to thank you very much for the wonderful day at Hibs. Please convey my gratitude to Tommy Hart and tell him what a relief it was to escape to a civilised football ground where all that terrible fucking swearing that goes on at English grounds isn't bloody well tolerated.

Secondly, I apologise for the behaviour of these two irrepressible Cockneys, Len and Kevin, who wangled their way to the game. Fortunately, as they speak a different language, their frequently insulting remarks were not understood by their neighbours in the stand. They thoroughly enjoyed it and have asked me to express their thanks to you and Tommy Hart. As they support Millwall, a team with a goalie and ten cloggers, they hardly ever witness any football: more like having a seat at the Battle of Stalingrad.

Lastly, as you are now aware, my worst fears about Willie Ormond's choice for the World Cup have now been realised. He is almost certain to play Holton or McQueen. Holton will be sent off after 5 minutes: McQueen might last 20. Not normally a betting man, I'll give you 3:1 (in large Scotches) that Scotland lose to Zaire in the first game. Draw: no bet: we buy our own.

Thanks again Ted to you and Jean. See you soon.

                    Yours sincerely,
                          Sandy Brown

Mr. Ted Glendinning,   11th June 1974
Edinburgh

Dear Ted,

             Scotland   10   Zaire   15

This is to confirm that a wager has been made regarding this game.

1. £1.00 worth of refreshment (winner's choice) is wagered on the result of this match: sounds like 2 × large Gin & Tonic or 3 large Scotches.

2. My 3× large Scotches says Zaire will win: yours says Scotland will.

3. Draw—no bet. I'm glad we've got that clear. You drive a hard bargain Ted.

                    Yours sincerely,
                          Sandy Brown

~ 8 ~

The Planning Game

Along with football, there was a number of recurrent themes that triggered Sandy to unleash unexpected emotions. Among these was Town Planning and its Officers, or 'jumped up sanitary inspectors' as he referred to them.

Immediate Records Ltd.,   12 January 1969
W.1.

Attention of K. Mewis Esq.

Dear Ken,
   I enclose a letter to the Planning Officer who suddenly got stroppy today.
   I'd have preferred to go round and land one on him, as he told us things were going to be O.K. before, but instead I find myself writing a grovelling, forelock-touching letter like this. That's the way the fucking cookie crumbles: no wonder I'm taking pills.

Yours sincerely,
Sandy Brown

His architectural career was interspersed by confrontations with Planning Authorities, and his frustration with what he saw as unnecessary controls often resulted in semantic arguments such as 'can sound recording be classified as an industrial process when the product is altering a few electrons on a piece of tape'. His attitudes were summed up in a paper given to the Oxford Society of Architects.

THE PLANNING GAME

As I'm expecting a large sum to be offered by Waddingtons for this harmless and diverting amusement I will preface my exposition of it—and the attendant fatuous remarks I shall make—with this vital symbol '©'.

Let me tell you how the idea came to me. I was watching Q.P.R. playing a goalless draw, of which they played many last season before they discovered that running about kicking the ball rather than opponents cheered and excited their supporters, when a deep calm descended upon me like a vulture. It was beyond boredom. Unfortunately, later in the season the games became of interest and I was unable to reproduce this pleasing catalepsy. I turned to cricket, but, on television, this is usually limited to Sunday matches with the outcome almost certain to be a win for one of the teams. Test cricket of course is much better, but it's hard to get five days off to watch it and I was really looking for a game that could take years rather than days, and one that I could play professionally.

Suddenly: a gestalt. Planning! If only it could be codified properly it would knock Monopoly for six while evoking the kind of prolonged ennui necessary for the elusive catalepsy found briefly in the goalless draw of football.

A great deal of groundwork had already been done, culminating in the U.K. in the 1971 Act, the subsequent DoE Directive of November 1973 and the interim Dobry Report—all three of them happily contradictory documents. And I had produced my own 'Brown's Index of Tidiness' at a discourse I gave to the R.I.B.A. in 1972. This bears repeating as no one paid any attention to it whatsoever. Its basis was that statutory planning processes are divorced from economics, and as this means that Brasilias will generate shanty towns where the economic resources of a country aren't up to Brasilias *without* shanty towns, statutory planning processes should be connected to an index of tidiness.

$$\frac{n \sqrt[3]{A}}{P}$$

where A = Area available for development

P = number of inhabitants (population)

n = G.N.P. of environment in dollars per day.

In Calcutta, for instance, the index is unity = 1 sq. m. per person. If the planning laws stipulate more area than that for any development in Calcutta the laws will simply have to be broken elsewhere in the near vicinity. Hence shanty towns on the edges of Calcutta, São Paulo, Brasilia and so on. Although you end up with a simple space figure it's derived from available economic resources. The index for parts of California approaches 1000 m^2 per person, so the U.S. Federal Environmental Protection Agency can impose fairly stringent conditions there without generating an inequitable problem.

The index for the U.K. is only 130 and in central urban areas 75, so, if the G.N.P. continues to drop in real terms—as it did in [19]73, the index will drop below the threshold provisions of the 1971 Act in the worst hit areas. There are signs in Notting Hill Gate that this has already happened and that enforcement of the Act will therefore simply redistribute slums as in Glasgow and Edinburgh. As not every clause in the [19]71 Act has yet been fought in the courts it's impossible to pinpoint what the Act, together with the proposed new Building Bill, sets as a threshold. But we may be close to it.

You can see this is very exciting stuff, and I detect some eyelids are even now dropping. Good. There's plenty more.

1. Firstly, the time element. I've said that a 5-day test match is hopeless in terms of time. The 1971 Act says that the Planning Authority have two months *or* 59 days at least, and 60 on leap years. One of the months would have to be February. NOTE: get your planning applications in during January of any year—saves a day. Or if you're playing the game avoid February at all costs.

2. Secondly, if, as is usual in central urban areas, the Planning Officer asks for more time, this will be done on a form which doesn't tell the applicant *how much* more time: it could be forever if the applicant agrees. For the purpose of the game, then, it's important to agree to 'further time'. If, on the other hand, the Planning Officer *doesn't* ask for further time, the applicant has no legal alternative but to appeal to the Minister. Let's look at *that* time in central urban areas:

2 months + appeal (12 months) = 14 months.

Hardly the kind of catalepsy-including schedule I'm looking for, *but* if one accepts the DoE circular and the interim Dobry Report we can spin the time out by *talking* (or as it's usually called 'consulting') with the Planning Officer. The average tenure of a post by a Junior Planning Officer in central urban areas is 4 months. So in any given situation of 'consultation' lasting 2 years you could be dealing with 6 consecutive planning officers. Good thinking in order to prolong the game.

The audacity of those who claimed to have researched formulas for the future that would avoid the follies of the past always aroused Sandy's cynicism. Another planning document— 'Broadcasting in the Seventies'—generated an outline for a new television series and an unpublished letter to *The Times*:

David O'Clee,   4 June 1970
Television Centre

David,

Now that the Silbury Dig is over, I feel that the time is ripe for the '100 Years of Portland Cement' series. It had been my original intention that this series would actually take only 100 years (5200 weekly episodes each 120 minutes), but after reading 'Broadcasting in the Seventies' I feel it may be necessary to slow it down a little so that the subject can be displayed in depth—one could hardly hope to adequately describe a slurry pit or the famous slump test incident in two hours.

What I propose is as follows: I and my scenario advisers (J. Cassels and R. Ordish) attend a meeting with yourself and Huw Wheldon to discuss the project. Knowing how important 'visuals' are to programme people, I will bring along a bag of cement and a jug of water.

Let me know when you're ready.

Sandy Brown

The Editor,
The Times,
E.C.4.

Sir,

Choral Evensong Etc.

While grave misgivings about the future of broadcasting are being expressed in your correspondence columns, it seems that these are exclusively concerned with the 70s; little or no thought being given to the long-term consequences. It is beyond reasonable doubt that during the 80s and 90s the whole of our 70,000 square miles of land surface will be covered by cement, and that, by the turn of the century, cement will be cascading over cliffs at Dover, seeping into the Solway, and that this time should be chosen to place (??) in jeopardy the projected series, '100 Years of Portland Cement' would therefore appear rash, not to say irresponsible. The original concept of the series, due to start in 1982, was that the schedules in radio and TV would be adjusted slightly to allow a simultaneous 10-hour daily coverage of the subject on all channels. Rumour has it that now only 9 hours per day are to be allocated, and, disquietingly, that Sandy McPherson's daily half hour at the concrete organ is to be axed—this at a time when the last few hundred tons of slurry for the great instrument are still setting in the moulds at the Jubilee Chapel. We, the undersigned, are unanimous in . . . (cont. P. 498)

～ 9 ～

Piss-ups

Although many of us will take some comfort in the medical opinion that it played no part in his demise, Sandy's propensity for refreshment, alcoholic, that is, was legendary. As Peter Clayton put it, 'he gave the impression that the world's vintners and brewers should not go paupers to their graves.'

The etymology of the term 'piss-up' appears in a correspondence with Sir Ove Arup and a partner in his Dublin office, an old friend of Sandy's—Jock Harbison. Both Sandy Brown Associates and Ove Arup and Partners have offices in South Queensferry, a small Scottish village wedged between the splendid road and rail bridges across the Firth of Forth.

12th July, 1974

Personal

Sir Ove Arup,
Ove Arup & Partners,
South Queensferry,
West Lothian

Dear Sir Ove,
1. *Annual O.A.P. Piss-up at South Queensferry*
   While I was unable to remember much of this event, I'm assured by your indefatigable Dublin Partner, Jock (what a name to own in Dublin), that I enjoyed it. I also hope that you enjoyed our minuscule private piss-up at our office.
2. *Longevity*
   I regret to tell you that at 45 years, I was unable to display your energy on the dance floor. I will naturally take steps to rectify my pitiful performance.

138

3. *J. Harbison*
   A fine man—but dangerous when dispensing refreshments: I
   expect you, as a Professional, to curb his proclivities in this
   direction. Nevertheless, he managed, in a roundabout way (as
   befits the Irish) to prevent my assassination in Galway some years
   ago by a kind of diplomacy which I don't pretend to understand,
   but *must* respect.
4. *Your Wife*
   Please thank her for her forebearance during your (and my) party,
   and give her my regards.
5. *Next Giant Piss-Up*
   If Sandy Brown Associates have this on a boat on the Forth we
   will almost certainly all be drowned, but I am currently investigat-
   ing less hazardous possibilities. My report will follow.
   Thanks again.

Yours sincerely,
Sandy Brown

c.c. Jock Harbison

Ove Arup & Partners London

18 July 74

Personal

Dear Sandy,
    Thank you for your letter of 12th July.
    I am awaiting your report with anticipation and forebodings. I
suppose that Jock realises that with all the 'pissing' you do, your
intake must be kept up!

Yours sincerely,
Ove Arup.

Ove Arup & Partners Dublin

21 August, 1974

Personal

Sandy Avick,
    Your ochrous bannered gospel message to Sir Ove arrived while,
me, I was deeply embedded in Atlantic Mists below in Kerry. I got to
deep rumination, concerned that his honour might not get the drift

139

of your brilliant description of the Edinburgh occasion as a 'piss-up'?
What is zis sing, you say—a piss up?

The Concise Oxford Dictionary she say piss is 'not now in polite
use'. Does up make it beautiful? So? If a Giant Piss Up is a large
beautiful piss (not polite) I think I'm for it! It should of course
include Binns Bowder Spring Ward and Burd so to speak to have a
pisspective or a pissometric at no extra charge.

Yours sincerely,

J. H. Harbison.

27 August 1974

Attn: Jock Harbison
Ove Arup and Partners, Dublin

Dear Jock,

Perhaps you and His Holiness would not object to my bringing to
your attention the elsewhere widely held view that the C.O.D. and
O.E.D. are not reliable texts where modern English vernacular
abounds?

The U.B.D. (Underground Blackpool Dictionary), edited by S.
Brown, but regrettably out of print, lists the following items:

1. '–Up' (n) communal activity dependent on meaning of
   leading term—see 'balls-up' etc.
2. 'Piss' (n) (colloq) poor quality alcoholic beverage. 'Pissed'
   (V—adj.) afflicted by 'Piss' (see above). 'Hopelessly Pissed'
   (v. adj. phrase) overwrought, tired, over-refreshed.
   'Pissed out of one's head' (subjective clause) prone to
   irrational acts.

You seem to have Bowdlerised Dick Bowdler's name to 'Bowder'.
Could you have meant 'Bounder'? If so, I agree with the description.
I think this part of the exchange is now over—over—if you prefer.

Best wishes,

Sandy Brown

The pub was a second office, and clients, friends and acquaintances
alike were firmly guided through the portals of 'the nearest'.
The products of many years' work in this office were devoted
to ways of coping with the exasperating nature of B.B.C.
bureaucracy. Among them were two exclusive clubs, The

Association of Lunch-Time Endless Refreshees and the Monotony Club of Great Britain. The aims of A.L.T.E.R. were set out in the registration form circulated by Sandy:

You are invited to become a Fellow of the newly formed Association of Lunch Time Endless Refreshees. Please fill in the appended registration form:

1. I wish to become a Falter.
2. I enclose 4000 bottles of Gordon's gin as a nominal subscription.
3. I agree to abide by the rules of the Association.

RULES: 1. Fellows will fall down at lunchtime.
2. In the event that Fellows have got up again by the same evening, they will fall down again as quickly as possible. Judges decision is final.

Fellows had one recurrent problem: that in the shadows of all licenced premises, from the unknown to the familiar local, there lurked that special breed of person whose passion is to endlessly and boringly bend the ear. In order to seek out and cultivate the best of them, the Monotony Club of Great Britain was formed. Victims were unknowingly set up and encouraged to perform for members, who later compared boredom thresholds and analysed their skills in dealing with interruptions and diversions designed to quell their flow. Teams were picked and compared for form; international branches were planned, but the movement took a severe blow when Sandy tendered his resignation:

Roger Ordish

Dear Mr. Ordish,

Regretfully I must tender my resignation from the Monotony Club. Mr. Cassels will be writing shortly withdrawing from membership too. You will want some explanation. Briefly, I think we are in over our heads. Consider the following narrative which I believe to be a factual—if shaky—account of some events yesterday:—

Mr. Cassels and I were engaged, at approximately 13.00 hours on a routine inspection of the Dover Castle prior to mounting another of our pub-clearing operations: we came to the conclusion that this was a simple venue—the kind of place that five minutes of Bob Halpin could deal with easily. We concluded our business and settled down to enjoying some refreshment. Slowly a pervasive hooray voice began to take hold of our attention. It belonged to a man who was later to be described incredulously by Mr. Cassels as 'someone whom you wouldn't notice in a crowd'. This man (if he *was* a man or indeed human) addressed himself to a fading blonde lady who made no reply, during one stretch of narrative, for 25 minutes. The burden of his message could be synopsized like this:

The man (or being) pretended to be a cameraman. For undisclosed reasons he was climbing a peak in the Pyrenees. As each boulder, each pebble, each grain was described in chilling detail it became clear that we were listening to an international master. Mr. Cassels and I became frankly worried. Was some unknown team leader trying to put the frighteners on us? We began a close study to find a weakness: then I thought we detected a crack. After only about 20 minutes the top of the mountain was reached and the descent began. I turned to Mr. Cassels and said 'hullo: he's rushing it a bit'. 10 minutes later I knew that I was unfit to be in charge of a team. It was found, on reaching the bottom of the mountain that a camera had been lost: nothing for it but to go back up again . . . there were two possible routes . . . no camera . . . climb down again . . . next day . . . climb another mountain . . . camera, amazingly, spotted from top of other mountain . . .

Need I go on? Mr. Cassels and I, thoroughly unnerved, fled the scene. On leaving I noticed through the window that the being and his companion had settled into the seats we had vacated. This symbolism, and that of the camera which had gradually taken the mantle of the steaming tablets brought down from Mount Sinai, told me that our mentors are either ultra- or infra-human. I'm not going to find out. My resignation is tendered: please accept it quickly. I think it sensible advice to suggest that you disband the Club before you get broken too.

Perhaps we should have a meeting.

Yours sincerely,
Sandy Brown

The Monotony Club did succeed in providing a training ground for 'Interlaffs', a transatlantic exchange plan that still remains active. Its co-founder, Chris Curran, a protegé of Sandy and Flo's, deserted Britain for the green and lucrative valleys and the Blue Ridge mountains of West Virginia. After obtaining an honourable discharge from the U.S. Army for sunstroke, he set up a real-estate business with his college mate Jim Hobbs. Chris writes to Sandy with the news, asks if he knows of any houses to rent in Morocco, and seeks help for a young and nubile Interlaff. Sandy replies, and follows up with a salutary tale.

8th Sept. 1970

Spectrum,
Boyce,
Virginia, U.S.A.

Dear Sir and Madam,

We understand from your name that you are in the rainbow retail business and would like a small one for our lounge. We would like your assurance that the colours are fast, however, as we've been having a little trouble with the one in our garden which, irritatingly, seems to fade just as we're about to get the crock of gold out—which is what we wanted it for in the first place.

I believe there is quite a big beach stretching for about a thousand miles South West of Morocco but whether you can rent a house on it I'm not sure: they seem to be rather scarce—plenty of sand though. Would a fort do?

About the good-looking 22 year old girl who can't type, I think I can help. Is she any good at entertaining sea-faring men far from home? There are some vacancies for attractive girls in establishments near Buenos Aires docks. I believe the pay to be quite good and the duties so simple that they can be performed, as it were, lying on one's back. But perhaps you meant in England. The trouble is getting work-permits: I'll have a think about it though.

Meanwhile keep Interlaffs going: Flo is going to write a cosy letter soon. Come and see us.

Your Pal,
Sandy.

C. H. Curran Esq.,
Boyce, Virginia, U.S.A.

Chris,

It seems that a Virginian landowner discovered, on the return of his daughter from a European vacation, that he was threatened with the acquisition of a negroid son-in-law. This, as you know, could pose certain social problems in the Blue Ridge area, so it was perhaps understandable, if not forgivable in this enlightened age, that he chose to remonstrate with his offspring. She was unmoved by his argument and said, 'Father, my fiancé is an honours graduate in Greats from Balliol College Oxford, and is a fine man of considerable sensitivity and achievement in artistic fields; furthermore, his daddy owns most

143

of Africa and he is well placed to afford me a luxurious and civilised future. The least you could do is to visit him at his sumptuous Chelsea home overlooking the River Thames. There you could discuss your reservations about our proposed union.'

Seeing little alternative prospect, her father called upon the gentleman a week later and was immediately impressed with his host's courtly demeanour. The handsome young negro pointed modestly to a Van Gogh worth about $2m in his cloakroom and said: 'I take no credit for that: were I a poor man I would be unable to treat my guests to morsels of visual beauty such as I am fortunate enough to afford in my present position.' Nevertheless, it was clear from the high quality of the other numerous objets d'art in the mansion that the young man's taste was the result of penetrating studies into the deepest meanings of art. Over the Napoleon brandy a discussion arose on the importance the negro attached to the devious roles played by Joseph Bonaparte and Robespierre in the French Revolution, and the young man vouchsafed much more interest in this and other historical puzzles than in running his enormous cartel of copper mines. 'Although I graduated in economics as well as the arts', he said, 'I leave these matters to "X" (a former Prime Minister of England) who is my junior partner: he seems to be making a success out of it.' Cigars were lit and the Virginian moved to the enormous panoramic window to observe the sun setting over the River Thames. The negro followed him and, with an expansive sweep of his hand, said, 'And dat ober dere am de ribber.'

Your pal,
Sandy.

~ 10 ~

British Leyland Nigeria

On a business trip to Nigeria in 1974 Sandy learnt that the inhabitants of Calabar, capital of The South Eastern State, had great respect for the Scots, having been educated by their missionaries. When the plane had taxied to a halt on his next visit, Sandy appeared sporting a kilt, a dirk in his sock, blowing the bagpipes. He got the job. I say 'blowing', because not a note was heard, and those who attended Sandy and Flo's memorable Burns Night parties will confirm that Sandy could play the pipes. On his return to London, the office 'gofer' was dispatched to exchange them and a second pair were filled with bursting lungs, only to remain totally silent. Finally, Sandy wrote to the shop who also admitted defeat and refunded his money.

The Manager
London Instrument Shop

Dear Sir
Bagpipes
1. I can't get your bagpipes to work. I have been a pipe major and am currently a well-known clarinet player, so I think the fault is in the instruments.
2. Can you either (a) get someone to demonstrate that they (or at least one set) *can* be played, or (b) return my money. The law is quite clear on this as you well know. There is no question of *not* refunding money, as you apparently told my assistant, if the goods are faulty. I think it reasonable for you to get a piper in to check out all your bagpipes and give you his opinion, otherwise this will happen again and again. If, at the same time, this piper can demonstrate to me that *any* set can be played without busting a gut, fine. I'll have them.

Sounds fair to me—you've got my money and I don't have anything at all yet.

Yours sincerely,
Sandy Brown

It was during this visit that Sandy discovered one of his clients with a new Range-Rover, full of problems and with no spare parts of the right kind in Nigeria. On his return he wrote to Lord Stokes, at that time Chairman of British Leyland.

Attn: Lord Stokes
British Leyland Motor Corporation Limited
London
N.W.1   12 December 1974

Dear Sir,
British Leyland: Nigeria

1. I enclose a letter from Mr Tom Szabo who is Chief Architect for the South-Eastern State of Nigeria, a very influential man in West Africa.

2. You will see that the syntax and spelling could be improved (Szabo is a Hungarian) but the message is unmistakable. I visit Nigeria as a Consultant frequently and I endorse his views. The Range-Rover is a winner in Africa, as a vehicle. It is not selling nearly as well as it could because the servicing facilities are totally inadequate.

3. Now I know that your company has a number of problems at present but unless its vehicles can be sold, no matter whether the company is nationalised or whatever, it will go out of business. It's very galling for me, as a Briton, to see British products failing through default. What can I say to prospective buyers? I suggested to Szabo that he write to you direct in order to evoke some action. As far as he's concerned what he's got is an excellently designed vehicle which is just a heap of junk—and an expensive one—until he can get efficient service and spares at reasonably short notice. Patently he hasn't got this.

4. A personal note from you to Szabo, however brief, would work wonders, if followed by brisk restitution of the situation. Nigeria's economy has amassed $4.5 billion dollars through oil revenue in

the last 12 months. That's important. This letter cost me £5 to write, and I don't work for (or drive) British Leyland. I'd just like to see more British products in Africa: the Range-Rover is an obvious seller in that market. Make it work.

Yours faithfully,

Sandy Brown

British Leyland Motor Corporation Limited
From the Chairman and Chief Executive's Office

13th December 1974

Dear Mr. Brown,

Thank you for your letter of the 12th December regarding a Range-Rover in Nigeria. I have asked our resident Managing Director in Nigeria to look into the matter.

I do not think you are quite fair to say the vehicle is a heap of junk. Even from Mr. Szabo's letter some of the complaints are due entirely to extraneous circumstances.

We are very large exporters to Nigeria and, in fact, one of the largest in this country. We have our own office in Lagos and good distributors and dealers but I cannot comment on this particular vehicle without having the matter investigated.

Nevertheless I am very appreciative of your interest and would be glad to reciprocate when asked about the quality of British architects.

Yours sincerely,

Donald Stokes

From: Lord Stokes

Lord Stokes
British Leyland Motor Corporation Limited
London NW1   17 December 1974

Dear Lord Stokes,

Mr. Tom Szabo's Range-Rover: Nigeria

Thank you for your letter of the 13 December on this subject. It was extremely prompt and courteous: exactly what was required to reassure Mr. Szabo, whom I shall be meeting in Calabar in early Jan. 75. I will show him your letter. He will be delighted.

British Leyland Nigeria

The Range-Rover is an excellent vehicle, particularly suited to conditions in Nigeria. In order to forestall witty but barbed comment should you be asked about the quality of British Architects, my reference to a 'heap of junk' was over-reactive, offensive, ill-judged, and a number of other things, all totally reprehensible. I withdraw this idiotic allegation without reservation. Please try to forgive my stupid remark.

Yours sincerely,
Sandy Brown

Tom Szabo's Range-Rover was repaired in record time. During another visit to Nigeria, the Gowon government announced a far-reaching campaign to stamp out bribery or 'dash' as it is known locally. Sandy paraphrased the press announcement in his own release:

Translation

A message to the People from Admiral Browon:

De cabinet have been rackin de brains concernin de question ob dash. Dis country rapidly becomin laffin stock on account ob dis aggravated question and dat is de reason for de agonisin brain wrackin. After due considrashun an takin all de facks in account for benefitin peace unity an gainin respeck from de worl at large insted ob being that de clowns ob de peace we unanimous come to de conclusion dash mus go. So from now on no more dash on pane ob serious penalties. Insted we institutin system ob grachooities. Dese grachooities being strickly control to a maximum ob 50% in any single year huner per cent in two year an so on. One or two septions only namely 50% can be increase only on de word ob de person obtainin de grachooities. Dis will get us regainin respeck. Each person mus ask clearly 'gib me dis grachooity exceedin 50% cos of septional circumstance', den if de grachooity not bein paid de action up to ebry local bystander to act as court judge and jury. All dese officials to get de grachooities too. Abryone mus realise dat dis mus be proper judishl.

Admiral Browon

148

~ 11 ~

The Reaper

There is no doubt that Sandy knew the Reaper would shortly be visiting him. News from his brother that he and his aunt had glimpsed him too provoked this letter:

Professor James H. Brown,
Winnipeg, Canada

Dear Jimmy,
   Thanks for your letters of 11th and 16th October 1974.
   It's reassuring, in an age of uncertainty and high unemployment, that the Reaper is still hard at work, although I'm sorry he's been in touch with you again. His agility knows no bounds, as I've always thought him to spend most of his time on my doorstep: yet he appears, without invitation, 4,500 miles away. Peggy phoned (of course) and told me she had slight phlebitis. What is the Reaper up to? What's his game?
   You will note from the enclosed that I'm not known in E13—where I think I should now move to escape the Reaper's vigilance—and that I'm not E73 either. Perhaps you should utilise the postal code on our letterhead.
   The only good news is that, having phlebitis, Peggy is presumably unlikely to testify at the Watergate Trials. I've told her to take it easy and you know how much attention she'll pay to that advice.
   About the weather. December is a good month by your standards. Last time I was in Winnipeg in December my balls froze, severely curtailing subsequent peccadillos that I'd been planning for years. Cheer up. If you can make it to '76 you may be able to witness the collapse of civilisation as we know it.
                           Your old Pal,
                               Sandy

149

Two days before his death, working from the office in South Queensferry, he came across an advertisement in the local newspaper—'LOVED ONES BEING NEGLECTED?—If so, write or phone for details.'

Cemetery Landscaping Services,   13th March 1975
Edinburgh

Dear Sirs,
1. My Father is buried in a plot in a cemetery in Dalkeith Road. I've forgotten the name of it. His name was John Brown (which may take a bit of researching). We have, in our family, a title deed (freehold) to this plot and I don't expect Dad takes up much of it.
2. My Mother is elderly and may not live too long. Neither I nor my brother expect to make it too much further, although we've been saying that for at least ten years.
3. I expect Dad's grave is overgrown—I haven't visited it for 40 years. What I would like from you are the following:
   (a) Estimate for cutting the grass and generally clearing up the plot.
   (b) Maintaining it in reasonable—not good—condition, per annum.
   (c) Your assessment of whether you could get any more dead people on the plot. I will not be there: I've donated my body to the medical profession. I don't expect my brother to be interested: he lives in Canada.
   (d) Itemised costs for 3 (a), (b) and (c).
Yours faithfully,
Sandy Brown

This was his last letter. The reply came too late. Two days later he returned to London, and on a grey Saturday afternoon died in his bed, glass of Scotch to hand, watching Scotland lose to England in the Calcutta Cup.

~ 12 ~

Sandy Brown—a Discography

FOREWORD

A discography is a strict chronology of recordings made by a band or a musician. It lists personnel, dates, matrix numbers (where they have been allocated to individual titles by the recording company), tune titles and catalogue numbers. Originally I intended this listing to contain every known recording of Sandy Brown on tape, acetate or issued disc, but the business of collating broadcast transcriptions, private recordings—even television and film soundtracks—proved too great, and it was decided to restrict the discography to known commercial recordings (with the exception of the very earliest titles). Doubtless as soon as this appears in print someone, somewhere, will unearth recordings of Sandy thus rendering this discography obsolete; but that's show business . . .

Alun Morgan

Acknowledgements

Apart from the standard discographical works, notably *Jazz Records 1942–1969* by Jorgen Grunnet Jepsen (published by Karl Emil Knudsen, Copenhagen) and the now defunct *Discophile* magazine (edited by Derek Coller) I would like to acknowledge the considerable help generously given by the following: David Binns, Terry Brown, John Callis, Reg Cooper, Pete Moon, Don Tarrant and Kristov Zabrowski.

Abbreviations

The following abbreviations have been used in this discography:
Instruments: *alt*, alto saxophone; *bar*, baritone saxophone; *bjo*, banjo; *bs*, bass; *clt*, clarinet; *d*, drums; *g*, guitar; *p*, piano; *sop*, soprano saxophone; *tamb*, tambourine; *tbn*, trombone; *ten*, tenor saxophone; *tpt*, trumpet; *vcl*, vocal.

151

Record labels—all British unless otherwise stated:
Black Lion; CoE, Columbia; DeE, Decca; EncE, Encore; Esq, Esquire; FntE, Fontana; Mar ArchE, Marble Arch; MetS, Metronome (Swedish); MFPE, Music for Pleasure; Muza (Polish); Nixa; PaE, Parlophone, PyeE, Pye; RCA; S&M, Swarbrick and Mossman; Seventy-Seven; StvD, Storyville (Danish); TpoE, Tempo; One-up.

SANDY BROWN:

Sandy Brown (*p*); Drew Bruce (*vcl*)		Edinburgh—1948
	Emigratin' blues	private recording

SANDY BROWN'S JAZZ BAND:

Al Fairweather (*tpt*); Sandy Brown (*clt*); Stan Greig (*p*); John Twiss (*bjo*); Will Redpath (*bs*); Willie Burns (*d*).

Edinburgh—October 29, 1949

1049	Heebie jeebies	S&M unissued
1050	Of all the wrongs	S&M unissued
1051	Irish black bottom	S&M unissued
RS10–1	Irish black bottom	S&M 1002
1052	Melancholy blues	S&M unissued
RS10–2	Melancholy blues	S&M 1001
1053	Alexander	S&M unissued
RS10–3	Alexander	S&M 1002
1054	Of all the wrongs you've done to me	S&M unissued
RS10–4	Of all the wrongs you've done to me	S&M 1001

Note: 1049 to 1054 inclusive are ten-inch lacquer blanks while the items prefixed RS are single-sided master blanks. On S&M 1001 and 1002 Stan Greig's name is misspelled 'Gregg' on the labels.

Al Fairweather (*tpt*); Bob Craig (*tbn*); Sandy Brown (*clt*); Stan Greig (*p*); Norrie Anderson (*bjo*); Bill Strachan (*d*).

Edinburgh—November 11, 1949

125	Mandy Lee blues	S&M unissued
126	Georgia grind	S&M unissued
127, RS10–5	Willie the weeper	S&M 1003
128	Sobbin' blues	S&M unissued
129	Buddy's habits	S&M unissued
130	Buddy's habits	S&M unissued
131	Aunt Hagar's blues	S&M unissued
132	Keyhole blues	S&M unissued

133, RS10–6	I'm going away to wear you off my mind	S&M 1003
134	Canal Street blues	S&M unissued
135	Wild man blues	S&M unissued
136	Heebie jeebies	S&M unissued

Note: All the above were recorded on twelve-inch lacquer blanks but 127 and 133 were re-recorded onto master blanks and issued.

Add Jim Forsyth (*wash-board*).　　　　Stan Greig plays drums.
　　　　　　　　　　　　　　　　　　　　Edinburgh—May 3, 1952

159	Lady love	S&M unissued
160	Lady love	S&M unissued
161	Of all the wrongs you've done to me	S&M unissued
162	Jazz lips	S&M unissued

Omit Greig. Same session.

163	Jazz lips	S&M unissued
164	Krooked blues	S&M unissued
165	King of the Zulus	S&M unissued
166	Margie	S&M unissued
167, RS10–7	The Lord will make a way somehow	S&M 1004

Add Stan Greig (*bs*). Same session.

168	When you're smiling	S&M unissued
169	When you're smiling	S&M unissued
170	Jazzin' babies blues	S&M unissued

Note: All the above were recorded on twelve-inch lacquer blanks but 167 was re-recorded onto a master blank and issued.

SANDY BROWN (*p* solos):
　　　　　　　　　　Sandy Brown's home, Edinburgh—May 4, 1952

171	Maple leaf rag	S&M unissued
172	Maple leaf rag	S&M unissued
173, RS10–8	Weary Brown	S&M 1004
174	untitled original	S&M unissued
175	Little Rock getaway	S&M unissued
176	King Porter stomp	S&M unissued

Note: All the above were recorded on lacquer blanks but 173 was re-recorded onto a master blank and issued.

SANDY BROWN'S JAZZ BAND:
Al Fairweather (*tpt*); Bob Craig (*tbn*); Sandy Brown (*clt*); Dru

Peterson (*p*); Norrie Anderson (*bjo*); Dizzie Jackson (*bs*); Farrie
Forsyth (*d*).   London—July 11, 1953

RS399–2	Doctor Jazz	Esq 10–310	
RS400–2	Four or five times	—	
RS400	Four or five times	Esq 20–022	
RS401–1	Wild man blues	—	EP28
RS402–1	King Porter stomp—1	—	—

1, Stan Greig (*d*) replaces Forsyth.

HUMPHREY LYTTELTON AND HIS BAND:
Humphrey Lyttelton, Al Fairweather (*tpt*); Wally Fawkes, Sandy
Brown (*clt*); Bruce Turner (*alt*); Johnny Parker (*p*); Freddy Legon
(*bjo*); Mickey Ashman (*bs*); George Hopkinson (*d*).
                                    London—September 17, 1953

CE14702–7A	Four's company	PaE R3773, GEP8734
CE14703–5A	Forty and tight	unissued

SANDY BROWN'S JAZZ BAND:
Al Fairweather (*tpt*); John R. T. Davis (*tbn*); Sandy Brown (*clt, vcl*);
Alan Thomas (*p*); Mo Umansky (*bjo*); Brian Parker (*bs*); Graham
Burbidge (*d*).   London—April 1, 1955

VOG130	Everybody loves Saturday night vSB	TpoE A110, EXA13, StvD SEP312
VOG131	Too bad	TpoE A111 — —
VOG132	Something blues	— — —
VOG133	Tree top tall papa	TpoE A110 —

Note: All four titles also on Telefunken (G) VX4732.

AL FAIRWEATHER'S JAZZ BAND:
Al Fairweather (*tpt*); Sandy Brown (*clt*); Frederick 'Cedric' West (*g*);
Frank Clarke (*bs*); Stan Greig (*d*).   London—July 21, 1955

You're driving me crazy	CoE SEG7653
'Bye bye blackbird	—
Johnny is the boy for me	—
Blues slide—1	—

1, Fairweather plays slide trumpet.

SANDY BROWN'S JAZZ BAND:
Personnel as for April 1, 1955 session.   London—September 28, 1955

VOG240	African Queen	TpoE A124, EXA33, StvD SEP324
VOG241	Special delivery—1	— — —

VOG242   Nothing blues vSB TpoE A128   —   —
VOG243   Africa blues—2   —   —   —
1, Fairweather plays slide trumpet; 2, later retitled 'Blues Africa'.

Omit Davies. Concert, Royal Festival Hall,
                                     London—February 18, 1956
VOG621   Black six blues   TpoE EXA49, LAP8, StvD SEP334
VOG622   Blues stampede   —   —   —
VOG623   Fifty-fifty blues   —   —   —

Sandy's Sidemen:
Personnel as for April 1, 1955.   London—May 27, 1956
VOG854   Nobody met the train TpoE TAP3
VOG855   Candy stripes—1   —
VOG856   High time—2   —
1, Dave Stephens (*p*) replaces Thomas; 2, add Spike Mackintosh (*tpt*).

Al Fairweather's Jazz Band:
Al Fairweather (*tpt*); Sandy Brown (*clt*); Dave Stephens (*p*); Frederick 'Cedric' West (*g*); Major Holley (*bs*); Stan Greig (*d*).
                                   London—May 28, 1956
          Save it pretty mama   Nixa NJE1037
          Last minute blues   —

Sandy's Sidemen:
Personnel as for April 1, 1955.   London—June 21, 1956
VOG874   Swiss Kriss—1   TpoE TAP3
VOG875   Stay—2   —
VOG876   Mouseparty—3   —
VOG877   Look the other way—4   —
VOG878   My neck of the woods—5 —
1, Stan Greig (*p*) replaces Burbidge; 2, William 'Diz' Disley (*g*) added; 3, Bob Clarke (*vln*) and William 'Diz' Disley (*g*) added; 4, John Picard (*tbn*) replaces Davies; 5, Dick Heckstall–Smith (*sop*) added.

Al Fairweather Quartet:
Al Fairweather (*tpt*); Sandy Brown (*clt*); William 'Diz' Disley (*g*); Major Holley (*bs*).   London—July 10, 1956
          I'm in the market
            for you   Nixa NJT503, Met(S) MEP1106
          Chinatown, my
          Chinatown   —   —

DICK HECKSTALL–SMITH QUINTET:
Sandy Brown (*clt*); Dick Heckstall–Smith (*sop*); Dill Jones (*p*);
Major Holley (*bs*); Don Lawson (*d*).   London—August 20, 1956
                    Fish man   Nixa NJE1037
                    Monochrome   —

WALLY FAWKES–SANDY BROWN QUINTET:
Wally Fawkes, Sandy Brown (*clt*); Ian Armit (*p*); Lennie Bush (*bs*);
Eddie Taylor (*d*).   London—November 15, 1956
DR22668   Lullaby of the leaves   DeE DFE6379
DR22669   Bodger's blues   DeE DFE6378
DR22670   Polka dot rag   —

Same.   London—November 19, 1956
DR22738   As long as I live   DeE DFE6379
DR22739   Swingin' the blues   —
DR22740   Mobile blues   DeE DFE6378
DR22741   Avalon   —

Same.   London—December 10, 1956
DR22805   Lazy bones   DeE DFE6379
DR22806   Petite fleur   DeE J10855, LK4302
DR22807   Baby Brown   —
Note: Decca LK4302 also issued as Ace of Clubs ACL1154.

JOHNNY DUNCAN AND HIS BLUE GRASS BOYS:
Sandy Brown (*clt*, see note) with unknown group.
                                      London—*circa* early 1957
            Last train to San
              Fernando   CoE SEG773, DB3959, 45DB3959
            Ella Speed   —   DB3925, 45DB3925
            Jig along home   —   DB3996, 45DB3996
            Blue blue heartache —   —   —
Note: Sandy Brown is known to be present on one of the above four
    titles but it is not known which one. He may also be present on
    other Johnny Duncan releases from the period.

SANDY BROWN'S JAZZ BAND:
Al Fairweather (*tpt*); Jeremy French (*tbn*); Sandy Brown (*clt*); Ian
Armit (*p*); William 'Diz' Disley (*bjo*, *g*); Tim Mahn (*bs*); Graham
Burbidge (*d*).   London—March 5, 1957

Go Ghana	Nixa NJL9, NJE1056, Met(S) MEP1157		
The card	—	—	
Ognoliya	—	—	Met(S) MEP1158
Wild life	—	—	—
Monochrome	—	NJE1054	
Those blues	—	—	Met(S) MEP1157
Blues from Black Rock	—	—	
Saved by the blues	—	—	Met(S) MEP1158
Scales	—	Met(S) MEP1157	
Doctor Blues I presume?	—	Met(S) MEP1158	

Note: 'Go Ghana' also issued on PyeE GGL 0529 and 'Saved by the blues' on Mar ArchE MAL1167.

STAN GREIG'S JAZZ BAND:
Al Fairweather (*tpt*); Jeremy French (*tbn*); Sandy Brown (*clt*); Stan Greig (*p*); Al McPake (*g*); Tim Mahn (*bs*); Graham Burbidge (*d*).

Copenhagen—September 2, 1957

DGF166	Swingin' the blues	StvD A45047, SEP344, TpoE EXA90		
DGF167	Dreamed I had the blues	—	—	—
DGF168	Skinnie Minnie	—	—	
DGF169	St. James Infirmary	—	—	

Note: Al Fairweather and Sandy Brown listed on labels as 'Ali Badweather' and 'B. McDandy' respectively.

DICK HECKSTALL–SMITH QUINTET:
Sandy Brown (*clt*); Dick Heckstall–Smith (*sop*); Harry Smith (*p*); Brian Brocklehurst (*bs*); Eddie Taylor (*d*).

London—November 5, 1957

There will never be another you	Nixa NJT510
Sputnik	—

JOHNNY DUNCAN AND HIS BLUE GRASS BOYS:
Sandy Brown (*clt*) with unknown group

London—*circa* early 1958

Moanin' the blues	CoE 33S1129, EncE ENC190
Long gone lonesome blues	— —

SANDY BROWN:
Al Fairweather (*tpt*); Sandy Brown (*clt*); Bill Bramwell (*g*); Arthur Watts (*bs*). London—November 13, 1958

Portrait of Mies	Nixa NJL20	
Tipsy—1	—	
Sugar	—	

1, omit Fairweather.

AL FAIRWEATHER AND SANDY BROWN'S ALL STARS:
Al Fairweather (*tpt*); Tony Milliner (*tbn*); Sandy Brown (*clt, vcl*); Colin
Purbrook (*p*); Tim Mahn (*bs*); Stan Greig (*d*).

	London—January 18, 1959	
Maple leaf rag	CoE 33SX1159	
Up above my head vSB	—	EncE ENC159
Tidy	—	
Mountain music—1	—	
St Louis blues vSB	—	EncE ENC159
Careless love	—	
Fifth wind—2	—	One-up OU2092

1, omit Milliner; 2, omit Fairweather and Brown.

Same.	London—January 19, 1959	
Big Bill	CoE 33SX1159	
Gone to earth—1	—	
Old man river—2	—	

1, omit Fairweather, Milliner and Brown; 2, omit Fairweather and
Milliner.
Note: All titles on CoE 33SX1159 also on Met(S) MLP15024.

AL FAIRWEATHER:
Al Fairweather (*tpt*); Tony Milliner (*tbn*); Sandy Brown (*clt*); Joe
Harriott (*alt*); Bob Burns (*ten*); Cliff Townsend (*bar*); Stan Greig (*p*);
Jack Fallon (*bs*); Lennie Hastings (*d*).

	London—September 30, 1959	
Beat meat	CoE 33SX1221, Met(S) MLP15056	
Four or five times	—	—
Jim-jam	—	—
Sue's blues	—	—

ACKER BILK—CLARINET JAMBOREE:
Acker Bilk, Sandy Brown, Terry Lightfoot (*clt*); Fred Hunt (*p*); Bill
Bramwell (*bjo*); Jack Fallon (*bs*); Jackie Dougan (*d*).

	London—October 8, 1959	
Boodle am shake	CoE 33SX1204, SEG8053	
Slab's blues—1	—	

1, add Archie Semple (*clt*).

CLARINET JAMBOREE:
Sandy Brown, Archie Semple (*clt*); Fred Hunt (*p*); Jack Fallon (*bs*);
Jackie Dougan (*d*).　　　　　　　London—October 9, 1959

That old feeling	CoE 33SX1204
Louise	—

SANDY BROWN TRIO—CLARINET JAMBOREE:
Sandy Brown (*clt*); Jack Fallon (*bs*); Phil Seamen (*d*).
　　　　　　　　　　　　　London—October 9, 1959

The last Western	CoE 33SX1204

Note: All titles on CoE 33SX1204 also on MFPE MFP1045, Mar
ArchE MALS1375 and Met(S) MLP15038.

AL FAIRWEATHER AND SANDY BROWN'S ALL STARS—
DOCTOR McJAZZ:
Al Fairweather (*tpt*); Tony Milliner (*tbn*); Sandy Brown (*clt*—1, *p*—2);
Colin Purbrook (*p*—3, *tpt*—4, *tamb*—5); Brian Prudence (*bs*—6,
d—7); Bill Bramwell (*g*—8, *gong*—9); Stan Greig (*d*).
　　　　　　　　　　　　　London—July 6, 1960

Harlem Fats—1, 3, 6	CoE 33SX1306, SCX3367		
Oh dong bang that			
gong—1, 3, 7, 9	—	—	One-up OU2092
Wee Jimmy—2, 4, 6, 8	—	—	
Real sweet—2, 5, 6, 8			
(omit Fairweather)	—	—	One-up OU2092
Doctor McJazz—2, 5, 6, 8	—	—	

Al Fairweather (*tpt*); Tony Milliner (*tbn*); Sandy Brown (*clt*); Colin
Purbrook (*p*); Brian Prudence (*bs*); Stan Greig (*d*).
　　　　　　　　　　　　　London—July 8, 1960

Blues A	CoE 33SX1306, SCX3367		
The behemoth	—	—	
Al's tune	—	—	
Portrait of Willie Best	—	—	One-up OU2092

Denny Hutchinson (*d*) replaces Greig.
　　　　　　　　　　　　　London—October 10, 1960

Bimbo	CoE 33SX1306, SCX3367		
Glories in the evening	—	—	
The clan	—	—	
Monsoon—1	—	—	

1, Milliner, Purbrook, Prudence and Hutchinson

Same but add Bill Bramwell (*g*); Belle Gonzales (*vcl*).

	London—October 11, 1960		
Own up	CoE 33SX1306, SCX3367		
Monday vBG	—	—	
Belle's farewell vBG	—	—	
Two blue—1	—	—	One-up OU2092

1, Sandy Brown (*clt*) and Bill Bramwell (*g*) only.
Note: All titles on CoE 33SX1306 also on MetS MLP15064.

AL FAIRWEATHER AND SANDY BROWN'S ALL STARS:
Al Fairweather (*tpt*); Tony Milliner (*tbn*); Sandy Brown (*clt, vcl*);
Brian Lemon (*p*); Brian Prudence (*bs*); Benny Goodman (*d*).

	London—September 27, 1961		
Yaknik	CoE SEG8157, DB4769		
Blues march	—	—	One-up OU2092
Dinah vSB	—		
Wind of change (Akinla)	—		

Jackie Dougan (*d*) replaces Goodman.

	London—May 2, 1962
Caravan	CoE SEG8181
Portrait of Willie Best	—
Wall Street lament	—
Groover wailin'	—

FAIRWEATHER–BROWN ALL STARS:
Personnel as for September 27, 1961.

		London—July 2, 1962	
DR29556	Goosey gander	DeE LK4512, SKL4512	
DR29557	Morning glories vSB	—	—
DR29558	Wednesday night prayer meeting	—	—

BOB WALLIS JAZZMEN:
Bob Wallis (*tpt, vcl*); Keith 'Avo' Avison (*tbn*); Sandy Brown (*clt, vcl*);
Hugh Rainey (*bjo*); Brian 'Drag' Kirby (*bs*); Alan Poston (*d*).

	London—September 24, 1962
Didn't it rain? vSB, BW	PyeE 7NJ2060
In a little Spanish town	—
Up above my head vSB, BW	unissued

AL FAIRWEATHER AND SANDY BROWN'S ALL STARS—
THE INCREDIBLE McJAZZ:
Al Fairweather (*tpt*); Tony Milliner (*tbn*); Sandy Brown (*clt*); Tony Coe
(*ten*); Brian Lemon (*p*); Brian Prudence (*bs*); Terry Cox (*d*).

	London—November 20, 1962	
Quarterin'	CoE 33SX1509	
Wooden top	—	
Come Sunday—1	—	
Clarinet walk	—	
Toby	—	
Broadway—1	—	One-up OU2092
Wednesday night prayer meeting—1	—	—

1, omit Coe.

Sandy Brown, Tony Coe (*clt*) with same *p, bs* and *d*.   Same session
Satin doll	CoE 33SX1509

Omit Coe. Add Des McGovern (*g*).   Same session
Willow weep for me	CoE 33SX1509	One-up OU2092
Love for sale	—	

Sandy Brown (*p*); Des McGovern (*g*); Brian Prudence (*bs*); Terry Cox
(*d*).   Same session
Listen with Mammy	CoE 33SX1509
Main sequence	—

SANDY BROWN'S ALL STARS:
Al Fairweather (*tpt*); Sandy Brown (*clt*); Tony Coe (*clt*—1, *ten*—2);
Ron Rubin (*p*); Brian Prudence (*bs*); Terry Cox (*d*).

	London—September, 1965
Royal Garden blues—1	FntE TE17473
Stompin' at the Savoy—2	—
Love for sale—1	—
Work song—2	—

POLISH JAZZ—OLD TIMERS WITH SANDY BROWN:
Sandy Brown (*clt*); with Henryk Majewski (*tpt*); Zbigniew Jaremko
(*tbn*); Jerzy Kowalski (*clt, alt*); Tomas Ochalski (*ten*); Mieczyslaw
Mazur (*p*); Henryk Stefanski (*bs*); Marian Komar (*g*); Jerzy Dunin–
Kozicki (*d*).   Warsaw—October, 1968
B.M. rag	Muza LP30176
In the evening	—

Wiosenny spacer (Spring walk)   —
Blues dla Roberta (Blues for
         Robert)   —
Biale i cazarne (Black and white)   —
Zdrowie najwazniejsze (Health is
         first)   —
Hefi   —
Koszykarze (Basket ball players)   —
Blues dla dziewczyny (Blues for a
         girl)   —
Niepotrzebne skreslic (Unnecessary
         to be crossed out)   —

Incomplete Details
Beryl Bryden (*vcl*; Sandy Brown (*clt*) and the Old Timers Band.
                                     Concert, Warsaw, October, 1968
     No further details   Muza XL0501

SANDY BROWN AND HIS GENTLEMEN FRIENDS—
HAIR AT ITS HAIRIEST:
Kenny Wheeler (*tpt*); George Chisholm (*tbn*); Sandy Brown (*clt*); John
McLaughlin (*g*); Lennie Bush (*bs*); Bobby Orr (*d*); Brian Lemon (arr).
                                     London—Xmas week, 1968
     Ain't got no   FntE SFJL921
     Aquarius   —
     Black boys   —
     Easy to be hard   —
     Hair   —
     Underture: Where do I go?   —
     Hare Krishna   —
     Where do I go?   —
     Manchester, England   —
     Air   —
     Electric blues   —
     Overture: Where do I go?   —
     A final word from Mr. G. Chisholm   —

SAMMY PRICE—BARRELHOUSE AND BLUES:
Keith Smith (*tpt*); Roy Williams (*tbn*); Sandy Brown (*clt*); Sammy
Price (*p*, *vcl*); Ruan O'Lochlainn (*g*); Harvey Weston (*bs*); Lennie
Hastings (*d*).   London—December 4, 1969
     West End boogie   Black Lion BLP30130
     In the evening—1   —

Keeping out of mischief vSP   —
Struttin' with Georgia   —
In the evening—1 (different take)   Black Lion BLP30201
Just a lonesome babe in the wood   —
Royal Garden blues   —
Hungarian rhapsody   —

1, omit Smith and Williams.

Note: Sandy Brown does not play on seven more numbers recorded at
this session.

BRIAN LEMON ENSEMBLE—OUR KIND OF MUSIC:
Ray Crane (*tpt*); John Picard (*tbn*); Sandy Brown (*clt*); Bruce Turner
(*alt, ten*); Tony Coe (*ten*); Brian Lemon (*p*); Dave Green (*bs*); Bobby
Orr (*d*).   London—June 30, 1970

Straighten up and fly right   Seventy-Seven LEU12/38
Gentlemen of the bar   —
Sandy's blues—1   —
When my sugar walks down the
    street—1   —
I'm coming Virginia—2   —
After supper—2   —
Strike up the band—3   —

1, omit Lemon and Orr; 2, omit Coe, Turner plays tenor on 'I'm
coming Virginia'; 3, omit Crane, Coe and Picard. Sandy Brown does
not play on the remaining titles from this date.

SANDY BROWN WITH THE BRIAN LEMON TRIO:
Sandy Brown (*clt, vcl*); Brian Lemon (*p*); Tony Archer (*bs*); Bobby
Orr (*d*).   London—May 16, 1971

Ole Miss   Seventy-Seven LEU12/49
Oxford George   —
In the evening vSB   —
Ebun   —
Eight   —
Legal Pete   —
The badger   —
True love's heart vSB   —
Lucky Schiz and the Big Dealer vSB   —
Minstrel song   —
Louis   —

Note: Sandy Brown's clarinet is multi-tracked on 'Legal Pete', 'The
badger' and 'Lucky Schiz and the Big Dealer'.

PHIL SEAMEN—PHIL ON DRUMS:
Ray Crane (*tpt*); Gerry Salisbury (*cornet*); Keith Christie, John Picard (*tbn*); Sandy Brown (*clt*); Tommy Whittle (*ten*); Brian Lemon (*p*); Lennie Bush (*bs*); Phil Seamen (*d*).   Country Club, Hampstead, London—December 17, 1971

Allen's alley	Seventy-Seven SEU12/53
It's a wonderful world	—
When Sonny gets blue	—
Just squeeze me	—

CLARINET OPENING COPENHAGEN:
Valdemat Rasmussen (*tpt*); Ole Toft (*tbn*); Sandy Brown, Henrik Johansen (*clt*); Knud Fryland (*bjo, g*); Heinz Catstens (*bs*); Poul Jensen (*d*).   Copenhagen, April 16, 1973

Honeysuckle rose	CSA CLPS1009
Two sleepy people	—
Wild root	—
Pa tave bondes aget	—
The glory of love	—
New Orleans	—
You're driving me crazy	—
That's my home	—

EARL WARREN AND THE ANGLO-AMERICAN ALL STARS:
Bill Dillard (*tpt*); Eddie Durham (*tbn*); Sandy Brown (*clt*); Earl Warren (*alt*); Dill Jones (*p*); Major Holley (*bs*); Eddie Locke (*d*).   New York City—February 9, 1974

Undecided	RCA LFL.1.5066
Love for sale—1	—
Cold Monday blues	—
I never knew	—

1, omit Dillard, Durham and Warren. Sandy Brown does not play on one further title from this session.

Index

Index

Crocket, Stu 17, 38
Crosby, Bing 88
Curran, Chris 142, 143
Cuthbertson, Cubby 63

Dameron, Tadd 40
Dance, Stanley 39, 40
Dankworth, Johnny 100
Dare, Reggie 99
Davies, John R. T. 65–66
Davis, Miles 90
Deuchar, Jimmy 48
Diamond, Jimmy 96
Diamond, Peter 114
Dobell, Doug 64, 118
Dodds, Baby 60
Dodds, Johnny 35, 37, 38, 41
Dolphy, Eric 84
Dominique, Natty 36
Duff, Jack 17
Dutch Swing College Band 9
Dutton, Lyn 68

Eaton, Stu 17
Edinburgh Festival 89
Eel Pie Island 71, 72
Ekyan, Andre 98
Eldridge, Roy 40
Ellington, Duke 36, 40, 83, 93, 96, 101–
  103, 106, 113
Empress Hall 89
Esterson, Aaron 50
Esquire All Stars 91
Eysenck, Hans 53, 100, 101

Fairweather, Al 17, 18, 39, 44, 53, 65–
  68, 72, 73
Fairweather, Brown All Stars 122
Fallon, Jack 70
Fawkes, Wally 9, 15, 108
Fazola, Irving 97
Ferguson, Maynard 79
Fisher, Marvin 78
Fitzgerald, Ella 78
Five Original Blind Boys 41
Ford, Gerald 116
Fox, Roy 85
Franklin, Aretha 77

Garner, Erroll 78
Gelly, Dave 90
Gentry, Bobby 77
Gerhard, Roberto 83
Getz, Stan 47

Ghandi, Mahatma 16
Gillespie, Dizzie 40
Glazer, Joe 89
Glendinning, Ted 131
Glock, Sir William 92
Godbolt, Jim 122–129
Gold, Laurie 65
Gonella, Nat 84, 85, 89
Gonsalves, Paul 103
Goodman, David ('Benny') 54, 72–75
Goodman, Benny 35, 74, 91, 96
Gordon, Dexter 75, 98
Gordy, Berry 88, 97
Grade, Lew 92
Graham, Kenny 47
Grand Funk Railroad 41, 94
Granz, Norman 97
Green, Benny 105, 118
Greig, Stan 17, 70, 71
Gunning, Christopher 78

Hacker, Alan 35
Hall, Ed 67
Hamilton, Jimmy 107
Hammerstein, Oscar 83
Harbison, Jock 138–140
Hart, Tommy, 131
Hawkins, Coleman 40–47
Hayes, Tubby 102
Heath, Percy 75
Heath, Ted 29
Helm, Bob 37, 96
Henderson, Fletcher 101
Henebery, Terry 81
Herman, Woody 35, 43, 107
Hewson, Richard 78
Hindemith, Paul 83
Hitler, Adolf 16, 54, 84
Hodges, Johnny 36, 99, 103
Holiday, Billie 91, 97
Horne, Ellis 37
Horovitch, Ike 131
Horton, Roger 125, 127
Hucko, Peanuts 96
Hughes, Spike 85

Illinois State University Jazz Band 79
Ingham, Keith 48

Jackson, Dizzie 17
Jackson, Jack 61
Jackson, Quentin 93
James, Ruby 128
Jazz Centre Society 91, 114

Index

167